SPEAK, MY SOUL

LISTENING TO THE DIVINE WITH HOLY PURPOSE

MARSHA CROCKETT

SPEAK, MY SOUL: Listening to the Divine with Holy Purpose

Upper Room Books® website: upperroombooks.com

ISBN: 978-0-8358-2059-2
Epub ISBN: 978-0-8358-2060-8

Cover design: Faceout Studio, Jeff Miller
Interior design: PerfecType, Nashville, TN

Dedicated to
my husband, Ernesto Castro,
best friend, partner, and supporter of this writing life.
You make it easy to do what I love,
and I'm forever grateful.

CONTENTS

ACKNOWLEDGMENTS

Over the past several years, I've made new friends and connections through a number of online conversations. To all those who follow along on these digital streams, who find their way to my Soul Talk blog posts, or who subscribe to the Soul Talk newsletter, thank you for encouraging me in my writing and in my life in general. I pray that either in this life or the one to come, we can sit down face-to-face and share our virtual life in real time.

The team of professionals at Upper Room Books has made me so much better than I could ever be on my own. Thank you to Michael Stephens, Rachel Hagewood, Deborah Arca, Dylan White, and the entire team for caring, collaborating, and stewarding the words I offer here.

My family has faithfully nurtured me and encouraged my writing over a lifetime. Thank you especially to my sister, Linda Carlblom, who has been my first reader and editor on so many of my projects. To my daughters, Megan and Amy, thank you for your enthusiastic cheerleading of my efforts over the years. And thank you to my dear mother who faithfully asks every time we talk, "How's your writing coming along?"

And finally, to my husband, Ernesto Castro, to whom this book is dedicated. Thank you for your support and especially for designing and building with your own two hands my "Writer's Nest," where I find joy and inspiration to write. A writer couldn't ask for a better partner or a better expression of love on the journey.

To God Be the Glory.

INTRODUCTION

The soul speaks. Our God-breathed souls endow our human experiences with holy intention and purpose leading us on a path toward an intimate, dynamic relationship with God. If we are willing to listen to our inner voice, we are then better equipped to bear the image of divine love in the world. But we spend little time practicing the art of listening to our own souls talk. We don't always recognize the voice of our own inner being, let alone the voice of God. We are unpracticed in the art of deep listening to the rhythm of life, and we miss how God meets us there. We have few safe places to wonder and wander with others in the spiritual landscape of the soul. We don't take the time needed to struggle for our faith and wrestle with the angels, as Jacob did (see Gen. 32:22-31), asking God to reveal new identities and new pathways through our days.

I first recognized the possibility of my own soul speaking to me as I sank into the richness of the Psalms decades ago and listened to David and the other psalmists speak to their own souls. These same psalms became the dialogue Jesus used to express his own deepest human agonies, even as he hung from the cross. I continue to find rest and encouragement in these ancient songs. They offer me the freedom to explore questions, lament my troubles, and discern the presence and voice of God.

Speak, My Soul rests on this foundation of the Psalms inviting you to journey deep into your own inner life. On this journey through the inner landscape, we move through various stages on the spiritual path—not levels of accomplishments but pathways set in a circular rather than a linear progression. We may move around that circle from one path to the next, or we may journey across the circle from one side to the other. We often experience these pathways one at a time, or several pathways may merge into one. Only the Spirit can direct this journey. And while there are an endless number of pathways, here we will explore the pathways of Discernment, Discipline, Abiding, Wilderness, Identity, Community, and Contemplation.

Take your time as you work through these pages. You'll find seven weeks' worth of devotional reflections and suggestions for engaging in these readings, but give yourself the freedom to linger with a chapter or an individual meditation, to explore and sit with the invitations of the Spirit. This isn't a race, and it doesn't insist that you complete it perfectly in seven weeks. Take eight, or ten, or twenty weeks if that is your pace and preference.

And while we all do our own soul-searching, I encourage you to consider taking this journey in the company of other like-minded seekers looking for a deeper connection to the heart of the Savior. Appendix 1 offers a *Speak, My Soul* group leader's guide on how to start a listening group, explores each weekly topic more deeply, and provides information on active listening and group dynamics.

Each chapter focuses on one "inner pathway" and includes the following elements:

- A psalm—An opening verse and reflection acts as a trailhead marker for the week's sacred path. It sets the stage for the meditations to come and invites you to listen to your own soul speak.
- Six devotional readings—Daily meditations open your heart and mind to the various mile markers along each chosen pathway. The sixth reading focuses on part of the Passion narrative in the last week of Jesus' life.
- Rest Stops—Every journey must be balanced with places to rest along the way. Following each devotional reading, you'll find reflection questions or suggested practices designed to deepen your conversation with God and to prompt journaling.
- Soul Talk—On the seventh day, a weekly review and engagement brings together your inner-path work for your own personal

growth, to use in a small listening group, or in spiritual direction conversations. This review provides a suggested psalm reading and a guide for prayer and meditation through *lectio divina* (sacred reading).

Lectio divina is a slow reading of the scripture with a prayerful listening for the ways that your human experience intersects with the holy promptings from the Spirit. As you read, listen with the ear of your heart to any word or phrase that seems to draw your attention or resonate within you. This is a different experience than Bible study that focuses on contextual information, historical meaning, or research. This word or phrase that resonates with you is the prompting of the Spirit within your own spirit. Once you notice it, hold that word within your own heart and let it settle gently into your soul in the silence. Then slowly read the scripture passage once again. This time, listen for a divine invitation for you. Is there something to explore within? Something to release? An action to take or an attitude to address? These words become the way that God initiates the prayer dialogue. Respond to God in word or in the silence. Take a minute to record your word and your interaction with it in your journal.

As you listen to your soul on this journey, may you encounter the wisdom of the Spirit. May you learn to listen to your own soul as you travel the inner path and enter the welcoming presence of God.

Blessings on the journey,
Marsha Crockett
www.marshacrockett.org

THE PATH OF

DISCERNMENT

For God alone my soul waits in silence,
for my hope is from him.
He alone is my rock and my salvation,
my fortress; I shall not be shaken.

PSALM 62:5-6

Discernment is the practice of deep listening to the voice of God in its many forms. We rarely hear that voice in human words. But we may hear from God through a new awareness of the present moment or a desire of the heart that continues to call us to explore and draw closer to God. It may be an invitation to sit with a reality or a potential reality to see how it fits and notice what is life-giving and what is life-diminishing.

Discernment is difficult. We're often in a hurry or too distracted to sit and wait in silence for God. We like life to be resolved, to have no struggle that requires time and thought and prayer to get through the day.

We long for uninterrupted contentment, yet our very souls sometimes quake in turmoil as the Spirit awakens new invitations within. Learning to sit still and wait instead of wrestling against the silence calls for new dimensions of faith, especially in the suspense of unresolved realities. We often recognize the need for discernment when we arrive at a decision-point about something significant in life—a job, a move, a calling, a life partner, a change. While these big events do call for wisdom and seeking God's guidance, discernment as a path to hearing our soul speak asks that we look deeper into the heart of the matter. Here we listen and watch for the movement of the Spirit or the divine initiative and invitation in all aspects of our lives, not only the potentially big ones.

If discernment was simply about making the best-informed decision, then a list of pros and cons and confirmation from a wise source would be enough. But spiritual discernment asks for something more. Discernment is seeking to understand our desire to know God in a new way through an experience. Discernment is not like asking a question and then shaking a Magic 8 Ball to get an answer. Rather than looking for the right or wrong answer, discernment explores the path where we draw closer to God.

1. Discerning the Voice of God

If we are to hear our own soul speak, we need first to discern what the voice of God sounds like and to trust that we are perceiving the Divine initiative in our lives. The confusion comes when we attribute God's voice to other voices. As children, what we first heard from our parents is what we integrate as truth, even when that "truth" is false or abusive. Many other voices in our lives also interject their authority: an influential teacher, an overbearing pastor, an older sibling, or a dehumanizing boss. Sifting through the messages we have internalized—positive or negative—is a lifelong process.

Cultural ideals can also be mistaken as a godly voice, such as a work ethic that insists that we build ourselves by amassing possessions or wealth. Wealth in and of itself is not good or bad, but our focus on it can turn to idolatry. The rich man demonstrated this reality when he was invited to follow Jesus after selling everything he had and giving it to the poor. The scripture says "when he heard this, he was shocked and went away grieving" (Mark 10:22). The cultural messages can sometimes be more powerful than the ones we receive from people in our lives who truly care about us.

So what does the voice of God sound like? First, the voice of God is life-giving rather than life-diminishing. The voice of God is full of grace and mercy toward each one of us. "Surely I know the plans I have for you, says the LORD, plans for your welfare and not for harm, to give you a future with hope" (Jer. 29:11). This promise doesn't mean that life then becomes easy. When God calls Moses to go to Egypt, Moses has to confront challenges every step of the way, including his own negative self-talk. Yet the compelling voice of God continues to lead him toward freedom for the Hebrew people (see Exod. 3).

The voice of God is creative, always designing something new out of even the most difficult life circumstances. "If anyone is in Christ, there is a new creation; everything old has passed away; look, new things have come into being!" (2 Cor. 5:17). But creating something new is slow work, and we often dismiss these invitations because of the investment of time and attention it may require. Leaving a career and re-educating oneself in a new field takes time. Approaching the habitual dysfunction of our relationships and learning new methods of interaction takes time. It is a slow process to search for our own voice of the soul.

The voice of God respects our free will. Some people argue that we must crucify our will like Jesus does in the garden of Gethsemane (see Luke 22:42). But Jesus doesn't pray to kill off his own free will but rather to strengthen it to enable him to choose the path God has prepared for him. The choice remains squarely within his hands whether to offer up his life for the love of God or to turn and exert his own self-will to avoid the pain of the moment. There is a difference between self-will—based in the ego—and free will—based in the soul. Free will is the seat of the soul and is necessary if we are to choose to love.

Learning to discern the voice of God is possible, and it is the deepest desire of God's heart to be in intimate conversation with each of us. When we are willing to listen to the divine invitations, we enrich the pathways of life.

REST STOP

In what facets of your life are you discerning the voice of God? How do you recognize the Divine voice within? What other strong voices can you identify in your life that sometimes entangle themselves with the voice of God? How have you responded to the invitations of God? Is this a time to wait on God or a time to move forward, to name your gift, embrace a call, and give expression to it in some way? Journal your responses.

2. Discernment in Everyday Life

If discernment is a spiritual practice, then how do we experience it in our everyday life when we are simply moving through the ordinary tasks of our days and week? Most days there are no big decisions looming, no disasters to deal with, only small movements, adjustments to routines, intersections with others, energy expended in work and play, and times of resting.

One daily practice of discernment is called the Daily Examen. This practice is simply a time when we invite the Spirit to sift through all that the day has given. We notice what was life-giving or life-diminishing in some way. We consider how God spoke or drew closer in it all.

Beneath this prayer is a foundation of trust that makes it possible to come boldly before God in the first place. We all use different words or expressions for what this foundation feels like. For me, this foundation of belief includes trusting that God is always at work and is reaching toward me with goodness and tenderhearted compassion. And it includes my belief that Jesus is the greatest example of how to live out God's compassionate grace and truth in this world.

With this foundation firmly in place, I begin to review my day, not necessarily minute by minute but gently allowing thoughts to arise from my day: the morning, the afternoon, the evening. I notice what catches my eye. I pause to consider those moments and what the invitation may be. Are there habits or attitudes that need to change? What is the evidence of Divine presence in that encounter, that emotion, that thought? How might it lead me to God's goodness and compassion for me or for others? How does it inform my life going forward tomorrow?

This prayer becomes a pathway I share with God where we talk like intimate friends about what's happened or what hasn't happened. And as we do this over and over, the daily practice makes the discernment of the big life events and decisions a more natural conversation on a well-worn path with God.

REST STOP

If you've never done so, consider writing your own foundations of faith, the basis underlying your belief about how you live your life. If it feels too overwhelming to do so, approach it as a list of words that expresses what you value about your spiritual life or how you experience God. How do you react to the idea of partnering with the Divine to review your daily, ordinary life? Does it feel inviting, invasive, impossible, or some other response?

3. Hearing, Seeing, Touching

Henri Nouwen describes discernment like this: "Discernment is a life of listening to a deeper sound and marching to a different beat, a life in which we become 'all ears' . . . . Discernment allows us to 'see through' the appearance of things to their deeper meaning and come to know the interworking of God's love and our unique place in the world."[1] Discernment is the process of looking for God's fingerprints on our lives, looking for God's footprints on our path, and listening for God's thoughts in our minds. It does take some practice to discern that voice and touch of God, versus the strong human voices that may have formed and shaped our lives over the years.

Notice how Nouwen speaks of hearing and seeing. And I would add the sense of touch as well as we consider the fingerprint of the Divine in daily life. Discernment is a sensory experience—though we may never hear the literal voice of God or feel the physical touch of God, we experience the tangible results of God's presence in our lives. Discernment involves being open to that presence and tuning all our senses to be ready to experience it.

Beyond the questions of listening, looking, and feeling for God, there is a reciprocal question: Do I want to be heard or seen or touched by God? It's a question Jesus often asked individuals before speaking healing words into their life. "Do you want to be healed?" Or "What do you want me to do?" It's one thing to say *I want to know God.* But it's another thing altogether to agree to be known by God. When we pray to know God, we must often begin with the divine invitation to know ourselves. It can take some time to unveil and remove the layers that surround the inner being—the self-protecting distrust, the self-preserving reputation, or the self-resistant power struggles.

The forming of the soul in coming to know our self and God is the work of the Spirit within us. While we are invited to show up and observe and listen to that work, we don't actually do the heavy lifting. It is the Spirit that works within us. Discernment is this never-ending relationship of listening and being heard, of seeing and being seen, of touching and being touched by the faithful, ever-present love of God.

REST STOP

Find ten or fifteen minutes to sit quietly, to close your eyes, and to imagine Jesus sitting with you, calling you by name and asking, "What do you want me to do for you?" As he sits with you, notice how your body, mind, and spirit respond to his presence and his question. How do you want to respond? What questions arise within you about knowing and being known by God? Capture your response in your journal.

4. Discerning Purpose

Even as a full-fledged adult, I sometimes wonder what my life is all about. What is my purpose in life? A friend recently said to me, "I don't feel like I have any dreams for my life." Our life's purpose is a big question, an important matter of prayer. But it's easy to get sidelined by simply surviving in this world. The routines of work, relationships, and activity keep us on the move and perhaps entertained, but somewhere along the way, we may have lost our ability to dream beyond our current constraints. We naturally want to feel like we are contributing in a meaningful way to the world, or at least to our family and friends. But this pinpoint purpose often eludes us. Discerning purpose in life typically is a slow unfolding, but three elements lead us on the path of discernment.

Belovedness—When discerning our purpose or calling, one of the main components we consider is God's will for our lives. And of course, the question always arises, "How do I know I'm doing God's will?" When I shifted my focus from *doing* God's will to simply *being* God's will, I began to trust my own living, breathing experiences in this world. And to know I am the will of God means to know I am beloved by God. This knowledge gives greater purpose to every minute of my life. Wherever I am and whatever I am doing, I am living out my God-given vocation because I am living from my identity as God's beloved.

Inner Wisdom—There are clues to our purpose built into our DNA. They come to life in our experiences, personalities, preferences, passions, gifts, and talents. This inner wisdom is something we may downplay because the experiences of life feel so "ordinary." It takes time to be able to look deeply into life, to consider the arc of a life story and the themes scattered across the decades. Even simple things—like noticing the types of books we read, the movies we're drawn to, the things that bring joy—are all clues to finding open doors to unique opportunities that we alone are equipped to fulfill. The wisdom of a purposeful life is hidden within the soul.

Delight—The movie *Chariots of Fire* immortalized the Olympic runner Eric Liddell. Liddell had a most unorthodox method of running, almost flailing through the air to win race after race. And while his story revolved around his commitment to honor the sabbath by not running his Olympic race on his set-aside sabbath day, what really compelled him was this: He felt the delight of God on him when he ran. We've each likely (hopefully) experienced moments when we felt like we were in the flow of divine delight: a moment in which we thought, "I can't *not* do this!" It may be solving a problem at work, rocking a child to sleep, breaking out the paint and brushes, or hiking along a beach at sunset. The opportunities to experience God's delight on us and within us are endless. These moments draw us into our purpose of existence.

As we begin watching and listening for evidence of our belovedness, our inner wisdom, and the delight of God stirring within us, we more easily discern the inner path that enlarges our dreams and our ability to live with holy purpose.

REST STOP

Respond to the three elements considered to discern purpose: Belovedness, Inner Wisdom, and Delight. Which have you experienced? Where do you long to discern and confirm God's will or purpose in your life? Use your journal to explore each of these aspects of a purposeful life, both what you've experienced and what you're longing for.

5. Holy Discontentment

Wrestling with faith often involves confronting doubt, not to pin it to the ground and suppress it but rather to take it by the hand and allow it to open a door that leads to a broader unfolding of what it means to have faith. Often we experience doubt as something that begins to unsettle our settled-ness. We may respond to it with defensiveness to protect what we've claimed to believe in the past or what we claim as our own faith tradition. We may dig in our heels and become more resolved and redouble our efforts with spiritual disciplines. We may also exhibit judgment if we realize that a new truth in our faith journey aligns with those whom we've disparaged in the past. Yet the doubt persists. Until we get honest with our own souls, we will continue to feel the tension of our emerging faith.

The doubt—or, as I like to think of it, the holy discontentment—may feel like the irritating sand in the oyster but may eventually become a beautiful pearl. How can discontentment be holy? It's holy when it leads us to deeper water. It's sacred ground when we grow dissatisfied with easy answers that sound hollow when we're thirsty for a *hallowing* of ordinary life. When we sense something more that invites us to explore, learn, take another step, simplify, and cast off what encumbers the soul, we are sensing the Divine.

I wish I had a list of easy answers, a checklist to help me know that this is the way to walk with God. But the cadence of faith and rhythm of life are unique to each one of us. Yet we need not walk alone. We are given one another to walk alongside as we keep our eyes fixed on the Giver of Life and Faith. We are simply called to trust our experiences with God on the faith journey, which includes learning to trust that the annoyances, the discontentment, the defensive reactions are all keys to knowing a new facet of God-with-us.

Allowing the doubts and questions a seat at the table may feel uncomfortable. There is a vulnerability in giving voice to wondering curiosity. And always there is a holy tension in the unknowing, of not having an immediate resolution. But when we encounter this holy discontentment in ourselves and learn to take a breath and wait in the discomfort, we grow to have a deeper trust in the slow work of God.

REST STOP

In your journal get specific about your faith and faith practices. Where do you feel a tension in what you've understood about God or about faith in the past? Take a minute to name the tension and simply hold it in stillness before God. While you may not be able to say *all is well in this part of my soul,* consider acknowledging *all is held.* Trust that God is holding you safely in this season of discernment.

6. The Shadow of the Cross

Often as we discern our direction in life, we look at our options and make our list of pros and cons, and whichever one makes the most sense, we move in that direction. There's nothing wrong with that. But there is also another option to consider—the one that puts us in the shadow of the cross. The path of suffering will never make sense on a pro-con list, but it may be the place to which we are being called. Perhaps we are discerning an unclear path, one where we may not see clearly beyond the next step, yet we recognize the open door inviting us in. We may feel called beyond our own abilities and experience, beyond anything we could have imagined. Or maybe we feel led to a place that seems "beneath" us, not enough for us. It is only by faith and in the strength of God that we could walk on a path that will lead us to crucify ego, reputation, status, or well-earned authority.

This is the path that Jesus chooses. Before the crucifixion of the body, he makes a choice, a discernment of whether he can fully crucify his own self-will and physical desire in order to exert his free will that allows him to chose to follow the divine path set before him. In Gethsemane he can see what suffering lays before him. And death by crucifixion may feel beneath the dignity he deserves as the Son of God, or beyond what he can possibly endure. Yet, he sets all that aside and moves toward the shadow of the cross. Somehow, he finds the courage and fortitude to go on, to take another step closer. And as he does, we draw closer to God, closer to the hope of our souls.

Regardless of our circumstances or status in life, we all, at one time or another, face the cross. We encounter Jesus in our places of wounding, in our suffering of the soul due to loss of health, or loved ones, or ways of life. We face the cross as we mourn and rage against what is. We don't have to go looking for a cross to bear; it is ingrained into the reality of life, survival, injustices, and betrayals.

The question to discern is do we follow or do we turn and leave? Do we worship? Do we weep? Do we continue the long journey or continue on our own way? How do we find our way to sit faithfully in the shadow of the cross and commit our spirits into the hands of the Faithful One?

REST STOP

Consider a time in your life when you or a loved one suffered, and it felt like a burden too heavy to bear. In that place, imagine Jesus sitting with you, looking at you, working with you to carry the load. What do you see or hear? What do you want to say to him about that time in your life? Now imagine Jesus walking the road to his crucifixion. In that place, imagine joining him, looking at him, working with him to carry the load. What do you see or hear? Sit in the shadow of his cross and say what you need to say about your suffering.

7. Soul Talk

For personal reflection, spiritual direction dialogue, small group discussion, or on retreat

Lectio Divina: Psalm 62:5-12

Slowly and prayerfully read aloud the scripture passage above describing how David practiced discernment and listened for the voice of God. Listen for a word or phrase that resonates or catches the attention of your heart. Hold that word or phrase within you during a minute of silence. Now, slowly read the verses again, listening for deeper connection, invitation, or guidance related to the word or phrase. What is God saying to you through this scripture passage in this time and place?

After another period of silence, journal what you've received, heard, or longed for. If you're with a group, briefly share the word and your reflection from this reading with one another, listening without comment or the need to give advice or even agreement. Simply hold the divine words received in safe and welcoming silence.

The Inner Path of Discernment

- If you journaled through each of the six readings, go back and review your journal entries. What thread connects your

thoughts? What is the prevalent theme of your reflections? How might that thread be woven into a prayer?

- If you haven't journaled, simply reflect on the readings. What has stuck with you? What rises as important for your own journey? What words or thoughts did you underline?
- How were you challenged with the idea of spiritual discernment?
- How have you sought out discernment or practiced discernment in your daily life?
- What invitation are you sensing related to discerning the will of God?
- What might you need to release or adjust to practice discernment?

Receiving Grace

What grace or gift do you most desire from God as you consider the invitation to spiritual discernment as a doorway for drawing closer to the Divine?

THE PATH OF

DISCIPLINE

O God, you are my God; I seek you;
my soul thirsts for you;
my flesh faints for you,
as in a dry and weary land where there is no water.
So I have looked upon you in the sanctuary,
beholding your power and glory.
Because your steadfast love is better than life,
my lips will praise you.

Psalm 63:1-3

As we travel this journey of learning to listen to our soul speaking, we may long for new expressions and practices that allow us to draw close to God. Psalm 63 identifies several forms of discipline that teach us to acknowledge and name our heart's cry: to gaze upon God, to witness God at work, and to offer praise. These practices invite us to journey deeper on the sacred path within.

In considering the path of discipline, it's important to remember what *discipline* is and is not. We can understand *discipline* as akin to *disciple*. Spiritual discipline is the work we are called to as disciples of

Christ. Spiritual discipline is not the means by which we get God's attention. God is all eyes and ears for us long before we learn how to respond. Nor is spiritual discipline the work we do to make ourselves grow. Only God brings about transformation and spiritual growth. Spiritual discipline is the sacred path that puts us in a posture of receptivity. It prepares our thirsty soul for the living God.

God is constantly revealing things to us and inviting us to explore facets of ourselves and our faith that will inspire stronger discipleship. Spiritual discipline leads us to offer a holy "yes" to what God is offering. God has paved and prepared the path ahead. All we need do is walk on it.

So in prayer or praise, in silent stillness or loud busyness, in work or rest we walk the sacred path of spiritual discipline.

1. Missing Worship

Recently I realized that I'm missing worship. Even as I expressed that thought in my journal, I wondered what exactly I meant by it. All I knew was that when I was in church or in my quiet morning time set aside for prayer, I somehow felt distracted and distant from God. I remembered what worship used to feel like and look like, but somehow something had changed within me. Whether we worship communally or privately, prefer the silence or the music, choose a soaring stone cathedral or the cathedral of nature's making, we all worship. It's part of what defines the human experience. But what's at the heart of worship?

As I explored the idea of worship, I knew that I had lost my focus on worshiping God in my everyday life. I believe my ordinary experiences and interactions are the holy ground where God shows up. But worship isn't only about what I'm receiving from God. It's more than evoking a spiritual feeling or a fleeting emotion. Worship is something I offer to God as I realign my heart, mind, and spirit to focus on who God is.

When I worship, I release my self-reliance and embrace the reality of God as the source of all life. I let go of thinking the world—or my workplace or my family—can't get along without my being available 24-7, always ready to receive a text or a call and to respond immediately to every inquiry. Worship strips away my presumption that what I contribute and produce in this world is connected to my worth. In God alone my identity rests. So while God is always reaching toward and pursuing each of us, worship enables us to reach toward and pursue

God. We turn our hearts toward God to know and honor the Divine One among us.

Psalm 63 calls us to look upon God in the sanctuary, beholding the power and glory of God. How do we do this? The sanctuary certainly refers to the holy gathering place of God's people, but we also know that our souls are God's temple and dwelling place. We are called to behold God's presence within us. All creation also bears the glory of God. We see God in the divine tenderness of the tiny sparrow as well as in the majestic canyons or deep-rooted ancient forests. The glory of God is in the awe-inspiring realities of this life and this world—from the details of how the body orchestrates life to the endless varieties of flower and fauna, to the mysteries of the interconnectivity of all creation. The sanctuary of God is far-reaching, and, at the same time, it is as near as our next breath.

REST STOP

Spend an hour or a day set apart to worship God in a new or different way than a traditional worship service. Let your worship inspire you to sing, dance, shout, work, play, and pray. Do it all to the glory of God.

2. Intentional Discipline

Discipline of any sort is always an expression of something greater than the discipline itself. Financial disciplines represent fiscal priorities and goals I set for myself. Physical disciplines address my desire for health. And spiritual disciplines reveal my willingness and desire to be in relationship with God. Disciplines call for intention, as they give structure to my desire in how I order my hours, my days, my life.

Viewing spiritual discipline as a specific method or program to knowing God misses the point. That isn't to say that we shouldn't jump into a practice of prayer or meditation or devotional reading. All these attempts to connect to the Divine express the desire to do so, and this in itself delights God. But we can view spiritual discipline not in terms of how well we practice a discipline, or how successful we feel in it, but rather as an offering of time and space to yield the heart, mind, body, and spirit to divine love.

This offering is not a way to earn God's attention but rather a portal into the soul that acknowledges God is already present and working. It recognizes the need and desire to be led by a love that we cannot create on our own. It trains the soul to recognize the voice of God, to consider all of life in relationship to God, and to release all that may hinder this connection.

In my practice of spiritual disciplines, some days all I can muster is to simply show up to the possibility of a God connection. So I come as I am—weary, distracted, busy-minded, giddy, resentful, rushed, or tenderhearted—it does not matter. I simply come. Foundational to showing up is identifying a time and a place to do so. It doesn't have to be a room or a corner only used for prayer and Bible reading. The time and place may be a morning walk through the neighborhood or a coffee shop bustling with activity. Each of us can find our best time and the best place to offer ourselves to this divine work.

Wherever and however we are, we come, day by day, week by week, as months turn to years and years to decades of continually and intentionally turning the heart toward God. Sometimes we hear or sense the sacred promptings of the Spirit. Other days we simply recognize the longing in the silence that may feel like a void or a hunger. But all that we turn in the direction of God, whether emptiness or fullness, becomes prayer and nurture for the soul.

REST STOP

Take a few minutes to meditate and journal on the ways you've engaged in spiritual disciplines in the past (prayer, meditation, Bible study, worship, journaling, etc.). When and where do you show up? If you don't have a set time and place, identify one now. How have the spiritual disciplines brought life and deepened your desire for God? When have they felt like a burden and a drain on your time and energy? How do those disciplines intersect your ordinary life? What does the greater longing or hunger for more of the Divine life within you feel like, look like, sound like?

3. Soul Tending

This spring my tulips didn't do well. "Failure to thrive" is what I called it. After three years of stunning, strong tulip beds, this year they just didn't have the right conditions to reach their potential. They were only half the height. Some never bloomed at all. As I've researched, I've heard other gardeners say we've just had too much rain, even by Pacific Northwest standards. My research also told me that tulip bulbs actually have a fairly short life expectancy. Most regrow only two or three years and then need to be replaced.

I also am aware, however, that I haven't tended to the flower beds like I should. Grass from the nearby lawn overran the tulips, and I just haven't taken the time to deal with it. The soil hasn't been fertilized, and I haven't added new soil in years. Friendly squirrels love to dig up the dirt and occasionally a bulb from this flower patch. For many reasons, I can't blame my tulips for their lack of growth.

All these plant-life realities for my tulips also tell the story of the soul. Unless we tend to the health and growth of our own souls, listen to the inner voice asking for nurturing, care for the new seeds that have been planted, and show up to the work that needs to be done, we simply won't grow.

Spiritual disciplines in and of themselves don't make us grow, just as a gardener cannot make a seed grow. But we can tend to the conditions of body, mind, and spirit like a gardener tends to the conditions of the garden, shaping a safe space where growth can occur. We steward our God-given lives. At times the body may call for more rest or more exercise. The mind may call for releasing old habits or expanding thought patterns. The spirit may require time for stillness, meditation, or creative expression through music, art, or literature. The more we pay attention to the conditions of our beings, the more growth we will experience.

The tending is continuous, and it can be hard to see our incremental progress, our small growth. But sometimes what happens in coming to a spiritual discipline is life-changing. In these moments, faith becomes clarity of purpose, thoughts become action, sufferings or elations both lead to a welcoming peace, chaos disperses leaving wisdom for the path ahead. Then I know that I have been in the dwelling place of God found within my own body, mind, and spirit. "The word is very near to you; it is in your mouth and in your heart for you to observe" (Deut. 30:14).

REST STOP

In your journal, write the word *Body* at the top of the page. A third of the way down, write the word *Mind*. And a third from the bottom, write the word *Spirit*. Between each heading, write out words or phrases related to the disciplines you currently practice in each of these areas of life. *Body* might address both your own physical body as well as your physical environments, possessions, finances, etc. *Mind* encompasses your intellectual health, growth, learning, and what you feed your mind. And *Spirit* includes your emotional health, relationships, and faith practices.

Consider where you feel your life is longing for nurturing or support. In what areas do you feel stuck or withered? Which spiritual habits need to be replaced or renewed? What would feel life-giving to your soul today? How might that translate into a regular practice or discipline to keep your body, mind, and spirit healthy and centered within the love of God?

4. Grappling with Gratitude

Being grateful seems so common, so simple, so baseline to spirituality that it barely needs mentioning, except that . . . it does. Gratitude can easily slip away and be replaced by the temptation toward grumbling. The Israelites let their gratitude slip away in their wilderness journey. Instead of remaining grateful for their deliverance from slavery, they complain to Moses and Aaron about their conditions. They want to turn back to Egypt or to enter the Promised Land before it is time.

Recently I noticed a spirit of complaining had crept into my life. It's such a subtle intruder. It seemed wherever I was, I was mentally (if not verbally) assessing how a place or a business or an entire city could improve in appearance, operation, or outcomes. I was always on the hunt for better furniture for my own home, better dishware for the kitchen. Home improvement television and real estate sales apps fed my complaining spirit as I compared what I had to what others created for their own lives. My hunt for "better" was a subtle way of complaining that what I had was not good enough. It grew out of that spirit of discontentment.

To be honest, grumbling comes easily, especially when I'm in the workplace. It seems to be a natural response for me that I have to check and double-check. I often pray for God to put a guard over my mouth and my lips, to not let me get sucked into the dark alley of complaining about a boss, or another coworker, or the workload. Gratitude takes practice until it becomes the habit that forms my heart and becomes my natural first response. Gratitude isn't something to add to a list of spiritual disciplines. It's central to all disciplines. It anchors who we are in relationship to God. Even the psalms of lament are, in fact, grounded in gratitude for God's nearness and faithfulness throughout our lamentable lives.

Today, at this moment, I'm grateful for the technology that allows me to tap out these words, to send them out into the world as a small offering in thanks for the faithfulness of God. I'm grateful for the morning birdsong I hear; for the cool morning; for the earth abloom with the glory of violets, daisies, and hydrangea seen out my window; and for the challenge of the work that lies before me today. Lord, give me a grateful heart.

REST STOP

Throughout your day or this week, make note of the times you catch yourself complaining. Jot them down in your notebook or journal. At the end of the week, consider how your awareness of this attitude or habit impacted you. How might you incorporate gratitude as a regular discipline to replace the grumbling? Where do you recognize the faithfulness of God, or does it seem absent during this season? Despite the difficulties you may be facing, what simple things in your life are you grateful for today?

5. Complicating Spirituality

All disciplines call us to holy attention through the body, mind, and spirit, whether we choose to spend a devoted hour in silence, or meditate on scripture, or read from a daily devotional, or go and serve the poor. But we can overcomplicate our spiritual disciplines by turning them into structures that become taskmasters. We may add practice upon practice, thinking if a little is a good thing, then more must be better. Yet eventually our practice feels like nothing more than burden.

Overcomplicating spirituality is partly due to the tremendous accessibility we have to an endless array of resources in a variety of forms. It can leave us dizzy with possibilities. We are easily confused when trying to determine the best choice, the best cause, the best answer for the troubled soul. We have the potential for spiritual overload, overinforming and tempting us to a new practice or perspective, and, as a result, tempting us away from the living God and the simple presence of divine love.

It's not easy to strip down to the soul, to "take nothing for [the] journey" (Mark 6:8), as Jesus instructs the disciples who go out to share the Good News in human form. The props we use to guide our spiritual lives may become our stumbling blocks if we lose sight of the giver of it all. In reality, all we need is a willing spirit and a listening ear. We may be left feeling vulnerable if we put away our journals, our art supplies, our prayer mats, our devotional books (even this one!), and all our other tools we call upon for soul-care. Yet in that vulnerability we become dependent solely and simply upon the grace of God to lead us and fill us. And this is a beautiful place to be.

Simplicity is foundational to all spiritual practices. To Martha, the overworked, resentful sister of Mary, Jesus says, "Few things are needed—indeed only one" (Luke 10:42). He never explicitly says what that one thing is, and he does not say that there is only one way, but he points to Mary's singular and simple focus—sitting and listening at his feet—as an example of a better way of being. Whether it's creating hospitality, meditating on scripture, or any other spiritual practice, there's really only one thing needed to be in partnership with Jesus—an open attention to God. And this is expressed in ways unique to every human soul, whether we are busy serving or sitting still and silent.

REST STOP

What is the condition of your spiritual practices these days? Have they become overcomplicated, demanding, or dry? What "props" might you need to set aside for a time to offer yourself more freely to the movement of the Spirit within you? What is the "one thing" that God is inviting you to consider today?

6. Watch and Pray

As Jesus wrestled to discern his own path forward in the garden of Gethsemane, he asked his disciples to practice another spiritual discipline: watching and praying. And because it was late and darkness was falling upon them, he asked them also to stay awake with him, to work with him in the spiritual battle of the will. It seems like a simple request, especially as they must have seen the turmoil written on his face. Yet they succumb to sleep instead. Jesus notes, "The spirit indeed is willing, but the flesh is weak" (Matt. 26:41).

To watch and pray and stay awake invites us to bear witness to another's life and need. And as we witness their journey, it's difficult to know how we are to respond to it, or even how to pray for it, so we too are tempted to brush it aside and tend to our own needs for comfort, rest, or food.

To watch and pray, we enter into something potentially uncomfortable for the benefit of the other, just as Jesus asks the disciples to come alongside him. It may mean sitting at the side of a deathbed or listening to a personal struggle—deeply and attentively listening, with no regard for how to respond or fix a situation or to rescue someone from their pain and suffering. Or it may be as simple as resisting the urge to change the subject to something more pleasant. As we stay with those who grieve—not just in their immediate loss, but a month, a year, a lifetime later—we stay awake with them. We watch and pray.

In being awake to another and bearing witness to their life, we become the eyes or ears or hands of divine comfort, and as we comfort one another, so we comfort the heart of Jesus.

REST STOP

As you watch and pray and stay awake with Jesus, where do you notice suffering in your world? It may be as close as a family member in your own household, or it may be the suffering you feel heartbroken over in the world. What would it be like if, instead of ignoring the pain or running from it, you sat there with Jesus and listened to him pray with you? What specific invitation do you sense in your soul about this suffering? Is it a change in the way you are responding? Is it an invitation to research how to get more involved with aid to a marginalized group? Notice if there is a tension, a push-pull, internally about staying with someone in their suffering. Bring that tension to Jesus, and continue to listen to the promptings of the Spirit. What word or words speak comfort or compassion as you sit in this place of discomfort?

7. Soul Talk

For personal reflection, spiritual direction dialogue, small group discussion, or on retreat

Lectio Divina: Psalm 63:1-6

Slowly and prayerfully read aloud the scripture passage above describing the psalmist's desire for God. Listen for a word or phrase that resonates or catches the attention of your heart. Hold that word or phrase within you during a minute of silence. Now, slowly read the verses again, listening for deeper connection, invitation, or guidance related to the word or phrase. What is God saying to you through this scripture passage in this time and place?

After another period of silence, journal what you've received, heard, or longed for. If you're with a group, briefly share the word and your reflection from this reading with one another, listening without comment or the need to give advice or even agreement. Simply hold the divine words received in safe and welcoming silence.

The Inner Path of Discipline

- If you journaled through each of the six readings, go back and review your journal entries. What thread connects your

thoughts? What is the prevalent theme of your reflections? How might that thread be woven into a prayer?

- If you haven't journaled, simply reflect on the readings. What has stuck with you? What rises as important for your own journey? What words or thoughts did you underline?
- How were you challenged with the practice of spiritual discipline?
- How has a spiritual discipline been life-giving to you?
- What invitation are you sensing related to spiritual disciplines?
- What might you need to release or adjust in your spiritual practice?

Receiving Grace

What grace or gift do you most desire from God as you consider the invitation to spiritual discipline as a doorway for drawing closer to the Divine?

THE PATH OF

ABIDING

How lovely is your dwelling place,
O Lord *of hosts!*
My soul longs, indeed it faints,
for the courts of the Lord*;*
my heart and my flesh sing for joy
to the living God.

Psalm 84:1-2

On the inner journey we acknowledge the soul's longing to be at home and to dwell with God—a place where our spirit feels at ease, unencumbered, safe, and at peace. Home evokes a comfortable sense of belonging, a rootedness of the soul. But what remains is a longing that may feel like a homesickness or as if something is missing. It may intensify into grieving for a tangible touch from God.

At times we may enter what's called a "thin place," where the metaphoric veil between heaven and earth becomes more transparent, and we can more clearly see or experience that eternal dwelling place within our own souls. We have a sense that we are finally home and long to remain and rest there. There we may discover divine comfort or the deepening wisdom of God's abundant grace as we enter a profound mystery of love beyond our human imagining. These thin places are typically only a temporary glimpse into the eternal dwelling place, given to minister to our hearts even as we inhabit the temporal world where we live out our ordinary days.

And it's here in the everyday-ness of life where we practice knowing God, who dwells so close at hand that we fail to see it because it is as near and present as breathing. A simple thought turned toward God becomes the connection to this abiding place, just as a glance to a loved one across a room invites an intimate, knowing connection.

That longing and connection to the Divine can happen in a quiet moment when we remember to pause and pay attention. Or it may surprise us and show up in the center of a stress-filled workplace sitting in front of a computer screen. Sometimes we experience it while communing with like-minded worshipers on a Sunday morning.

Regardless of how we sense the presence of God—whether in a momentary "thin place" experience or a moment of silent awareness on the path of abiding—the invitation always comes from God who welcomes us into a gentle, hospitable grace, making itself at home within our own souls.

1. Abide with Me

Last winter I woke up with the old hymn "Abide with Me" playing in my head. Maybe I should say the song had lodged itself not only in my head but also in my heart, calling me to pay attention to it. Just when I thought it had run its course and left me, it would return again. Even on a recent episode of one of my favorite PBS series, *Father Brown*, the song was sung in its entirety! Lines from that hymn haunt me:

> Fast falls the eventide; the darkness deepens; Lord with me abide . . .
> Help of the helpless, O abide with me . . .
> O Thou who changest not, abide with me . . .
> Ills have no weight, and tears no bitterness . . .
> I triumph still, if Thou abide with me . . .[2]

I'm stopping to listen more deeply, to give pause to what feels like a prayer, asking Jesus to abide with me, stay with me, as the disciples on the road to Emmaus ask, "Stay with us, because it is almost evening and the day is now nearly over" (Luke 24:29). I am drawn to this prayer because it isn't focused on how I can or should abide with Jesus (although he asks that I do). There's nothing I must do to earn the presence of the Christ or the grace of knowing God. Rather, this message tells me that Jesus comes to me and abides with me even when I fail to recognize him. In my ordinary life and in my persistent weaknesses, even when it feels like evening, as darkness deepens during times of sorrow, there is the abiding Christ.

How does Jesus abide with me and stay with me in it all? Often, when I am still and place my faith into the reality of Christ's presence, I imagine him in the midst of my chaotic thoughts and activity or in my boredom with my daily tasks. And rather than my asking him to come to me and inviting the Divine into my life, I realize that Jesus is already here, acting as the host, inviting me to come into my own life experience. I become the welcomed guest as he opens the door to his dwelling place deep within my own soul and meets my cry to "Stay with me. Lord, with me abide."

REST STOP

Take a minute to put aside this book or your journal. Simply pause to be with God. Turn your deepest longing toward God and begin a conversation about where you could use God's dwelling presence in your life. How do you respond to the idea of Jesus taking up residence in your daily life? How do the lines from the prayer-hymn "Abide with Me" speak to you today? Record your prayer and heart desire in your journal.

2. Abiding Words

Life-giving words are like a handful of seeds scattered across the landscape of the soul. And when the heart is fertile, like well-prepared soil, those few seed words send down deep roots and nurture the soul to grow into a fruit-bearing being. It's miraculous, really. Words come to us from what we read and hear, or they may already exist within us as an inner wisdom coming into its own light. When I read words of centuries past from the great writers, thinkers, seekers, and mystics, their words have the power to inspire, nurture, inflame, revive, fortify, and, sometimes, utterly change me.

For instance, I remember when I first read Richard Foster's words about prayer being the dialogue where God "welcomes us home: home to serenity and peace and joy, home to friendship and fellowship and openness, home to intimacy and acceptance and affirmation."[3] These words became seeds that took root and anchored me to understanding and further exploring the difference between having a prayer life and experiencing life itself as prayer. Those words gave me freedom in my praying and drew me closer to a more integrated life with God—less God-out-there and more God-in-here.

Certainly the sacred scriptures have planted life-giving words within to nurture, challenge, strengthen, and direct me. In the conversation between Jesus and his apostles the night before his death, Jesus talks a lot about abiding or dwelling in him, like the branches abiding in the vine. And he adds, "If you abide in me and *my words* abide in you, ask for whatever you wish, and it will be done for you" (John

15:7, emphasis added). Paul reminds us of this truth in his letter to the church: "Let the word of Christ dwell in you richly . . ." (Col. 3:16).

I've listened to people who worry about not reading their Bible on a regular basis, skipping a day here or there, fretting over what they may be missing or needing to learn. Yet most of these people have been steeped in scripture for years. These words of scripture that we have come to know and can recall at any time are living words that continue to work in us whether we perfectly complete a Bible reading plan. The word is "living and active and sharper than any two-edged sword, piercing until it divides soul from spirit, joints from marrow" (Heb. 4:12).

Once we have received the words in scripture or other words that point us to God we can trust that they continue to abide and actively live and speak, leading us to deeper wisdom within the soul.

REST STOP

Take a few minutes to reflect on the words that you live by and that have impacted your life. What words were taught by parents or teachers and have stayed with you your entire life? Are they life-giving words, or do they weigh down your soul and need to be released from your inner monologue? How do those words continue to speak to you even though you received them long ago? Write down the words that speak to your soul and that your soul speaks to you. Thank God for the life-giving words that abide within you.

3. Abiding in Prayer

Many years ago, I wrote a book about prayer entitled *Weaving a Life of Prayer*. It felt daring to contribute to the conversation about prayer. The paradox of prayer is that it is an incredibly personal and yet universal experience. Each person willing to share about their prayer life could convey a different sacred act of communicating with the Divine One. The way in which each of us approaches God is our way alone. And the way in which God reaches out to us is for each of us alone. God connects with us individually as the one-and-only us that was or ever will be created. No one else has the same kind of experience that we alone have with God.

Some call prayer watching and waiting; others call it mindfulness. Some pray in silence, stillness, longing, or just listening. Others prefer Centering Prayer, interceding prayer, or a simple cry for help. With humbled hearts, open hands, or bended knees, prayer in its many forms and voices delights the one to whom we pray. Regardless of our personal prayer practice, we all seem to long for more in our praying. It's a topic that often arises in spiritual direction conversations. And this is the longing of the soul described in Psalm 84, the longing for God's dwelling place, or abiding place.

So our conversation often begins by acknowledging that the longing itself is prayer. I like to imagine that our longing for God or for more in prayer is actually a reflection of God's longing for us. The Spirit plants that longing in the heart that compels us to embrace the Divine, to rest in the holy scriptures, to settle into the loving presence that eternally surrounds us each day. Whether expressed in our longing to know God, in a mindful recognition of our own breathing, or in the rhythm of our beating hearts, our praying happens more naturally than we know. All we need do is relax and abide in the ongoing flow of divine conversation in which we are already immersed.

REST STOP

Set a timer for three minutes, and do nothing but notice your breathing. Center your breathing into the loving Divine Presence surrounding you and dwelling within you. What is the longing in your heart as you breathe as an act of prayer? What do you want to say to God about what you need in your life of prayer? What might God be inviting you to in prayer? Explore this invitation in your journal.

4. Abiding Together

A devoted commitment to knowing God, self, and others requires what Eugene Peterson called "a long obedience in the same direction" in his book by the same title. I like this phrase because it speaks to the reality that is abiding. Our journey through life with God never ends and always begins. This is the Alpha and Omega of the eternal Christ who orchestrates the evolutions of faith moment by moment, day by day. And it is the work of the abiding Spirit within that continues to lead us on this sacred path.

The spiritual life may be personal, but it is a journey we never walk alone. Always God invites us to journey with others. In the Celtic tradition, that trusted individual who travels the spiritual path with another is called *anam cara* or "soul friend," someone with whom you share your inner being, your mind, and your heart; someone who listens without judgments and welcomes you with the hospitality of grace.

A regular commitment to abiding with others for me has taken many forms. I have a handful of women I would consider my *anam cara.* We share a sacred friendship even though we don't see one another regularly. I also abide within a faith community, where I may not know everyone deeply, but we share a commitment to practice our faith expressions together in worship. I typically also connect with a small group within that faith community where we can further explore our journey together and learn from one another. And finally, I have met monthly for nearly two decades for one-on-one conversation with a spiritual director who helps me attune to all that God invites me into in my everyday life.

Abiding together calls us to devote our lives to that long obedience and the slow work of knowing God and knowing ourselves even when we don't perceive progress. It's building a spiritual history together over the weeks, months, and years. Paying attention to the ongoing new mercies and faithfulness of God never gets old. Tending the Holy by regular habits of abiding with others has the potential to utterly transform a life not only today but also as we set out on a new path tomorrow.

REST STOP

Take an inventory of those in your life who are faithful to you and your spiritual journey. What does that inventory reveal to you about what you have and what you need in the way of an abiding soul friendship? How are you that faithful friend who abides with others? Thank God for those who have met you along the path of life. What do you need or long for to deepen your ability to abide with God, with self, and with others?

5. Abiding in Ordinary Days

Yesterday I made oatmeal chocolate chip cookies. I emptied the dishwasher and reloaded it again. I went with my husband to shop for new rain gutters. I looked at my calendar to plan the upcoming tasks for the week ahead. I answered emails and checked my social media channels. I repotted a houseplant. I made dinner. I watched a little TV. I fell into bed tired enough to be sound asleep minutes after my head hit the pillow.

Ordinary life defines the majority of our days. And in the midst of it all I sometimes wonder, *Is this it? Is this the most significant that my life will ever be? And where is God in this mundane existence?* Yet, as I look back and reflect and offer prayers of gratitude, I recognize the ordinary becomes sacred to the extent that I recognize and acknowledge the holiness of sharing a meal, the aroma of fresh-baked cookies, the interactions with nature, and even the places and times I rest.

The "holy ground" moments found in scripture always show up in the ordinary. Even Moses was in the midst of an ordinary day working for his father-in-law when he came upon the burning bush. Paul's blinding light conversion experience occurred as he was commuting to work. The miracle of feeding the 5000 grew from a child's lunch. And Bartimaeus's healing happened as he was sitting by the side of the road. All of it sounds familiar because none of it is too far from our own realities, and this gives me hope.

Intimately knowing God in everyday life is really the only way we can know God because life is nothing if not ordinary. Each of us must look for God's presence in our daily life. We are invited to embrace our life as prayer, to consider the desires of our own hearts, to discern what

God is saying in the midst of it, and to turn it all in the direction of God to use as tools to transform the heart, mind, and soul. May our bed-making, bread-baking, office-tasking ordinary life be the holy ground where we abide in the divine light each day.

REST STOP

At the end of your day, make a list of all the ordinary things you did. It may be a long list: making the morning coffee, taking a shower, dropping kids off for school, going to the grocery, commuting to work, taking a walk. Then choose one or two of those ordinary moments and meditate on them. Engage your senses to help you remember what you saw, felt, heard, smelled, tasted. Consider the richness of these ordinary moments, and look for the ways God met you there or is now inviting you to be more deeply aware of such moments tomorrow. How might a prayer practice of looking at the ordinary moments of your day make a difference in your life?

Wht are ordinary things you do

6. Abiding in Christ

"At once [Judas] came up to Jesus and said, 'Greetings, Rabbi!' and kissed him. Jesus said to him, 'Friend, do what you are here to do.' Then they came and laid hands on Jesus and arrested him" (Matt. 26:49-50).

Shocking. How can one who has lived closely and intimately with Jesus over the past several years stoop so low as to betray him in exchange for a few pieces of silver? We would be less shocked if one of Jesus' enemies like a Pharisee or one of the Roman guard finally got their act together and arrested Jesus or stoned him in the streets as they had tried to do on more than one occasion. But then it would not have been a betrayal but rather a political power move.

Even more shocking is that Jesus calls Judas "friend" at the very moment of betrayal. Betrayal comes when a confidence or trust is broken, when what was offered before is now withdrawn. While Judas withdraws his love from Jesus, Jesus never withdraws his love from Judas. Hours earlier in the upper room, Jesus knew that Judas would soon leave to eventually betray him, yet he welcomed him to the table, washed his feet, and served him the bread and the wine along with the others. Jesus remains with Judas to the end. The friendship is not forgotten or replaced by hatred or resentment or retaliation from the hurt of betrayal.

Jesus lives fully within the Divine will that so loves this world, even when we turn our back on that love. He goes to every extreme to continue to abide and stay with us on behalf of that love. He would even give his own life so that we might live and come to abide in that love.

Read

REST STOP

As you meditate on this radical grace that never forsakes you, how do you react? When have you witnessed or experienced this kind of grace and kindness that remains despite the action or the hurt inflicted by another? Have you had opportunity to abide with others who the world would say are undeserving of such kindness? How might this gift of abiding be an offering to others in your life, in your community? Are there boundaries to how and when you are called to abide or stay with others, and when you must leave a situation or person?

7. Soul Talk

For personal reflection, spiritual direction dialogue, small group discussion, or on retreat

Lectio Divina: Psalm 84

Slowly and prayerfully read aloud the entire chapter of Psalm 84, which opens with the longing of the soul for the place where the Lord dwells or abides. Listen for a word or phrase that resonates or catches the attention of your heart. Hold that word or phrase within you during a minute of silence. Now, slowly read the chapter again, listening for deeper connection, invitation, or guidance related to the given word or phrase. What is God saying to you through this scripture passage in this time and place?

After another period of silence, journal what you've received, heard, or longed for. If you're with a group, briefly share the word and your reflection from this reading with one another, listening without comment or the need to give advice or even agreement. Simply hold the divine words received in safe and welcoming silence.

The Inner Path of Abiding

- If you journaled through each of the six readings, go back and review your journal entries. What thread connects your

thoughts? What is the prevalent theme of your reflections? How might that thread be woven into a prayer?

- If you haven't journaled, simply reflect on the readings. What has stuck with you? What rises as important for your own journey? What words or thoughts did you underline?
- How were you challenged with the idea of abiding with God?
- What felt life-giving as you read?
- What invitation rare you sensing elated to abiding in God?
- How might you integrate abiding in God into your spiritual practice?

Receiving Grace

What grace or gift do you most desire from God as you consider the invitation to a deeper abiding relationship with the Divine?

THE PATH IN THE

WILDERNESS

In the day of my trouble I seek the Lord;
in the night my hand is stretched out without wearying;
my soul refuses to be comforted.
I think of God and I moan.
I meditate and my spirit faints.

Psalm 77:2-3

Even if we learn to abide and feel at home with the Divine, comfortable in the rhythms of our spiritual practices and finding life-giving purpose, we may abruptly come to a wilderness landscape that leaves us wondering if we took a wrong turn somewhere along the way. Often our first response is to redouble our efforts in the disciplines. But as we seek the Lord in prayer, we may still come up empty. We meditate on the Word, but our spirit faints for lack of nourishment, and we may begin to wonder what's true and what's real about faith.

At this stage of the journey, wondering and wandering feel like uninvited strangers on the wilderness path. But rather than looking at them with a skeptical eye, it seems the Spirit invites both the wondering and wandering to join the journey. When we face them and invite them along instead of running from them or ignoring them, they can ultimately lead us to deeper mysteries of faith that may feel barren in the beginning.

In the end, we come to know, whether in fertile fields or barren deserts, God is there turning "the desert into pools of water, and the parched ground into springs" (Isa. 41:18, NIV). And so we learn to dance in the desert and welcome this wilderness place with open arms.

1. Looking Beyond, Looking Beneath

For the most part, we live life on the surface. To a certain degree, it's how we are wired. We make a home, eat our meals, go to sleep, go to work, watch TV, answer emails, go for walks, drive the kids to soccer practice without giving any of it much thought. We operate on autopilot to perform these daily functions. And often we are able to find joy in the routines, comfort in the ordinary. Yet there are times the most ordinary actions begin to feel barren of meaning and leave us hungry for something more, something we can sink our teeth into, something to enjoy and savor more deeply, something we can point to as the greater meaning to it all.

Consider a single tree: We enjoy the shade, the fruit, and the beauty that we can see, but beneath the tree is an entire network nurturing, strengthening, growing, and grounding it. The same is true for us as we see and experience all that life offers us each day. From the outside, we may look like we're simply going through the motions. Yet beneath the most mundane routines, something deeper is occurring. If I take a few minutes to consider, I recognize God is present. So we look again, look beyond, look beneath, look above, and look inward for the holy ground, the burning bush, the sacred text written into the common condition of life.

Our spiritual ancestors give us examples of this kind of mindful looking in the midst of the ordinary. Brother Lawrence, a seventeenth-century kitchen worker who served a group of Carmelite monks and whose teachings were compiled in *The Practice of the Presence of God,* experienced the sacred in the midst of his work. "The time of business does not with me differ from the time of prayer; and in the noise and clatter of my kitchen, while several persons are at the same time calling for different things, I possess God in as great tranquility as if I were upon my knees in the blessed sacrament."[4]

This is not to say that every moment has to hold deep meaning. I need not overanalyze my existence. But an intentional "practice of the presence of God" allows me to sift out the day, to recognize the stream of life flowing beneath a barren land that leads me into simple gratitude for this present moment and circumstance, regardless of whether it feels dry, thirsty, or barren. This is our holy ground.

REST STOP

How do your ordinary daily activities sometimes feel like a place of wilderness? Where do you struggle to recognize the Divine in your daily routines? What practice might help you to look beyond, look beneath, look above, and look inward at what is going on at a deeper level? In your journal, record your observations and feelings about practicing the presence of God. What do you want to say to God about all this? What grace would you ask of God to help you in this?

2. Equinox of the Soul

Halfway through Lent, the spring equinox arrives—equal parts day and night. It seems an appropriate moment to pause as we move from the ashes and darkness toward the light and life on the horizon where resurrection awaits us. We move from a focus on knowing we are from dust and will return to dust one day. On this bridge between the darkness and the light, we find enough light to keep us moving toward hope, enough darkness to keep us searching for God in new ways.

Truth be told, most ordinary days feel like an equinox to me. There is always much for which to be grateful but always plenty to grieve over: the difficult condition of the world or just the condition of my own heart. Yet there is God reaching toward me. I find it amazing that God created both day and night, the darkness and the light. They each play a role to set the seasons in motion and give order to our days in the rising and setting of the sun.

Scripture tells us that God is light and within him there is no darkness (see 1 John 1:5). Yet the psalmist also says that God is wrapped in darkness (see Ps. 97:2), sometimes hidden from our sight, sometimes a mystery, sometimes simply present with us as we sit in our own particular times of difficulty. Nothing can separate us from God, not even our most troubling thoughts. God is able and willing to inhabit the brightest days and the darkest nights with us, to split our lives open at the right time to reveal God's presence. God is always working in our lives, as present today in life and chaos as God was at the dawn of creation and void.

Neither darkness nor light is a permanent condition. Always we are changing and our world is transforming. And while we may weep for a season in darkness, "joy comes with the morning" (Ps. 30:5). We turn again toward God on the horizon to make our way. We set our gaze toward an empty tomb on the path to find our own resurrection.

REST STOP

In what ways do you recognize both darkness and light inhabiting the same space within your life? Take a few minutes to imagine God sitting with you. What does that feel like, look like, sound like? What difference does it make in your life to live with this knowledge? How do you experience hope in the midst of the darkness?

3. Liminal Space

Over the past few months, I recognize that I've been living in liminal space—that space in between one thing and another. I'm just weeks away from retiring from a long career in communications. And while I continue to do my daily work physically, my mind and spirit are focused on the opportunities in the months ahead. I'm not fully in my everyday work, not fully in my retirement life, and I feel the tension, the push-pull of my heart to live out the commitment I've made to the workplace, while longing to more fully occupy my calling into my retirement years.

Liminal space is waiting space. It often feels like being stuck in nowhere. And if it lasts for a long period of time, it can feel like wilderness. In waiting, the challenge is to stay present to what is, to what each day offers, and to experience this in-between time as holy. Honestly, I have come to believe that all of life is in some form of liminal time. We wait for babies to arrive, for things to change, for the doctor to call with a report. We wait for growth to take place, for election results, for death to release a loved one's suffering. We wait for new seasons, for planes to arrive, for our turn in line. There is even liminal space that occurs in the nanosecond between inhale and exhale. Transition from one thing to another is simply our way of being. And rather than fight against it, we have opportunity to learn contentment in it.

Living in liminal space calls for living by *kairos* time. This is the word the Greeks used for time that was more than the *chronos* or chronological time that we mark off by the seconds and minutes. *Chronos* time asks *what time is it? Are we there yet?* These are the questions we typically bring into our times of transition or waiting. We want to get on with life. But *kairos* time asks a different question. *Kairos* asks *what is this time for?* There is meaning and purpose in this time, in the liminal space.

As I'm asking such questions of my own liminal space, I'm finding this time is for reflecting with gratitude on all that my career has given to me—how God has provided for my needs through it, how I've learned and grown and found meaningful relationships in the workplace. It's a time to offer prayers and blessing for my coworkers as they continue to carry on the work we've started together. And it is time to patiently wait for new seasons of life to unfold in their own unique way and time, trusting God to prepare the way ahead. Through intention, I am able to identify the sacred presence of God in my liminal time.

REST STOP

Take an inventory of all the in-between realities you are living today. Where are you waiting, moving from one thing and another? Consider whether you are pushing to leave the liminal time and places in your life or relaxing and trusting the timing to unfold naturally. As you wait, consider what this time is for. What is this season of waiting teaching you about God, about yourself?

4. Wilderness Time

At certain times throughout life we arrive at seasons that feel as dry as Ezekiel's valley of dry bones (see Ezek. 37:1-14). The inspiration and intimacy we once experienced when reading scripture now tastes like eating stale bread. The connection and growth previously experienced in a faith community suddenly evaporates. And praying about it feels like knocking on a door where no one is home.

When I find myself in the wilderness, I call to mind the truth of God's presence. The divine work eternally continues regardless of my perception of it. The Spirit moves with or without my understanding or any emotional connection. Even in what I perceive as dry spells, I believe I remain immersed, enveloped, and buried deep within the love of God.

There is no need to try to change how or when God may come to me or even reveal myself to me. Showing up each day in a posture of waiting receptivity during my desert times is an act of faith. I can trust the timing and the appearance of the Divine as it unfolds in me. As I sit and wait in this wilderness time, I consider the struggle with being here and how I want to move ahead. For now I simply grieve the loss of emotion or aliveness in sensing God's nearness.

I'm learning to have a deeper contentment in the silence of God, trusting it as holy invitation to partner in the silence as well. Here I recommit myself to trusting God's goodness without needing a sign or external proof of it. This goodness is planted like a seed in the darkness, waiting to mature and ripen in the soul.

I offer grace to myself on this silent path in the wilderness, never belittling myself or blaming my lack of faith for these road conditions. I slow my pace. I take time to observe, to find barren beauty in this desert landscape. And I'm careful not to call this path "solitary" because I'm comforted by the company of many other wilderness travelers who have gone before me—the saints of scripture like Abraham, Moses, Ruth, Elijah, and Jesus; the saints who followed through the centuries like the Desert Mothers and Fathers, John of the Cross, Saint Augustine; and those saints who live even into this generation like Mother Teresa and countless unnamed pilgrims who have walked this path and carry torches lit by the spark of wisdom and truth that leads us on. Together we learn to navigate this desert landscape.

REST STOP

During seasons of dryness it may be all we can do to practice the simplest spiritual disciplines that keep us from feeling frustrated or like we're working too hard to get God's attention. Instead, simply notice your breathing, remembering the breath of God living in you. Divine presence is the air we breathe. Nothing can be closer than the breath, the rise and fall rhythm of a God-breathed life. Spend a few minutes attuned to your breathing, recognizing it with gratitude as enough grace and gift for this day.

5. Lament, Longing, and Landing

With the latest horrifying news story or the still tender personal trauma inflicted upon our own lives, we cry out to God with unspeakable sorrow and mourn the losses that befall our human condition. While we weep we acknowledge our inability to guarantee a pain-free, harm-free future. We may cast blame upon individuals, organizations, political agendas, and even God as we long for divine intervention to restore our broken lives.

We have no answers to the "why" that accompanies the sighs. But if we stay with our sorrow long enough to listen deeply, we soon realize our lament is much more than just a complaint, much more than a wish for change. Lament is the voice of deep pain over what is broken in our world. If we listen still deeper, we hear the pain as a longing—longing for healing and wholeness, longing for restoration, longing for comfort, longing for new life. It is a longing for the promised kingdom of God.

When we bring our deep longing to the one who suffers with us and knows what it feels like to experience such pain, we find a safe place in the arms of the "God of all consolation" (2 Cor. 1:3) who hears and holds all our laments. Jesus himself prays in lament from the cross when he cries, "My God, my God, why have you forsaken me?" (Mark 15:34). When we pray our lament, we turn to the only one who can speak into our pain. We acknowledge our suffering, but we also rest with faith in the loving presence of God in the midst of our ruins.

The type of lament that juxtaposes pain with faith is rich within the psalms. "Why are you cast down, O my soul, and why are you disquieted within me? Hope in God, for I shall again praise him, my help and my God" (Ps. 42:5-6). "Answer me quickly, O Lord; my spirit fails. Do not hide your face from me . . . . Let your good spirit lead me on a level path" (Ps. 143:7, 10).

It is possible to hold both our lamenting *and* our comfort in the good Spirit that leads us back onto level paths. Lament is longing for the promised kingdom. Lament is also resting in the one who promises to bring such a kingdom. We can know both grieving *and* resting with faith in the one who carries us through. May our lament lead us to the only safe place we need to get through this moment of pain.

REST STOP

What communal grief or lament is occurring in your community or in the world today? Consider writing a prayer for community healing as a way to express this sorrow. In what circumstance or reality in your life are you personally grieving? How have you expressed that grief to God? How does your lament express a deeper longing in your life?

6. Following at a Distance

After Jesus is arrested, most of the disciples flee. Only two disciples remain. John records that he and Peter follow Jesus to the high priest's house. John is allowed in because he knows people inside. But Peter stays in the courtyard following at a distance. He warms himself along with some of the guards around a charcoal fire, hoping not to be noticed. But he is, and the questioning begins. "Don't you know the one they arrested? Aren't you one of his followers?" And the denials and the distancing of himself from Jesus begin.

When we warm ourselves by the fires of others, it's hard not to become like them. It's the peer pressure, the desire to play it safe, to fit in, to not be noticed that often drives us to say things we later regret or act in ways we're embarrassed to admit. There is safety in anonymity, where no one really knows what we believe, no one to hold us accountable if we denied truth or even a friendship. No one would be harmed. And we divide our own heart in pieces and wonder why we lost track of our faith and our Lord.

As the guards lead Jesus away, Peter watches from a distance, perhaps feeling the closeness of his Lord slipping away, wondering if life will return to what it was before Jesus invited him on this journey. Already feeling the absence of that divine strength, power, and lavish love that Jesus had poured out on everyone he met, questions have to be stirring within, likely the same questions we ask when we feel separated from Jesus and walk through a wilderness. *Where are you? Why have things changed? Is there something I'm doing or not doing that keeps me from hearing you?* But perhaps we are distanced by our own making.

Maybe it's just not convenient to follow Jesus' way. Or maybe the enjoyment of being busy in ministry keeps us from quieting the mind and heart and centering our attention on the Giver of life. Even though the distance feels real, we have this to hold firm to in faith because the distance itself speaks to the soul and reminds us that nothing "in all creation will be able to separate us from the love of God in Christ Jesus our Lord" (Rom. 8:39).

REST STOP

How would you describe your relationship with Jesus? Close, distant, indifferent, devoted, skeptical, or some other description? What are the realities that have kept you from knowing and following Jesus throughout your life? What might God be inviting you to consider as a means of drawing nearer to Jesus? How could you express all this in a prayer? Consider these questions, then listen for the divine, grace-filled response within your soul.

7. Soul Talk

For personal reflection, spiritual direction dialogue, small group discussion, or on retreat

Lectio Divina: Psalm 77:1-15

Slowly and prayerfully read aloud the lament in the scripture passage above and listen for the voice of God. Listen for a word or phrase that catches the attention of your heart. Hold that word or phrase within you during a minute of silence. Now, slowly read the verses again, listening for deeper connection, invitation, or guidance related to the word or phrase. What is God saying to you through this scripture passage in this time and place?

After another period of silence, journal what you've received, heard, or longed for. If you're with a group, briefly share the word and your reflection from this reading with one another, listening without comment or the need to give advice or even agreement. Simply hold the divine words received in safe and welcoming silence.

The Path in the Wilderness

- If you journaled through each of the six readings, go back and review your journal entries. What thread connects your

thoughts? What is the prevalent theme of your reflections? How might that thread be woven into a prayer?

- If you haven't journaled, simply reflect on the readings. What has stuck with you? What rises as important for your own journey? What words or thoughts did you underline?
- How comfortable are you in expressing your honest lament to God?
- What resistance or obstacle keeps you from prayerful lament?
- In the midst of your wilderness or transitional place, how are you finding ways to turn your heart and soul toward God?
- What is your image of God in the dry seasons? How does the Holy One meet you there?

Receiving Grace

What grace or gift do you most desire from God as you consider the path in the wilderness as a doorway for drawing closer to the Divine?

THE PATH OF

IDENTITY

You desire truth in the inward being;
therefore teach me wisdom in my secret heart.

Psalm 51:6

Deep within us lies the central essence of pure truth out of which our wisdom speaks. Here the voices that tell us lies about who we are cannot enter. *Soul* is the name of this inward being, the inner truth. After surviving the wilderness journey and after dwelling within God's transforming power opened through discipline and discernment, we arrive on the other side a different person—or perhaps just more attuned to the core of who we already are.

Here we come home to a place where we draw closer to the secret heart, the sacred true self where we are free to release our emotional ups and downs, to move beyond our circumstances and even our measures of success. We rest, silent and assured in who we are without need to defend or explain our divine, God-imaged self, even as we grow in grace, "transformed . . . from one degree of glory to another" (2 Cor. 3:18).

1. Finding True Self

The call to know ourselves and live from our "true self" is marked by a lifetime of learning to remove the masks that we would rather hide behind. When I was twenty-something, I decided I wanted to see what it was like to "live freely" as some of my friends seemed to be doing. So I went out drinking and dancing and hanging out with people I really didn't know. The choices I made were uncomfortable to me, and I soon realized this was not the life I wanted to live. And rather than living "freely," my choices, in fact, narrowed my world and left me feeling lonely and empty. I began again to rediscover who I was in new ways.

There's an interesting phrase in scripture that speaks about living an authentic life. The Gospel of John reveals Jesus as the Word made flesh, and it says that "he came to what was his own" (John 1:11). That phrase always stops me and invites me to meditate on its meaning for Jesus and its meaning for my own life. What God gives us to claim as our *own* includes the location, family, culture, and communities that become the landscape of how we live out our days. But it is more than our GPS location. It also means that we come to that which is true to who we are, how we are wired, and the God-endowed image of self in the context of all creation.

Finding our true self is easy to talk about, but how exactly does it happen? Each individual's journey to their true self is unique, but as we come to know God, we come to know ourselves. As I've explored and unraveled some of my own mystery of true self, here is what I've noticed:

- My true self considers the messages and values received from birth and takes time to consider if they are life-giving and truth-telling about my life as an adult at this moment.
- My true self examines life each day to reflect and ask questions. By what priority have I lived today? Where did I try too hard to prove my worth? How did I offer grace to myself in a difficult situation?
- My true self explores the false identities I've created in response to others' judgment of parts of me as bad, wrong, or inappropriate.
- My true self seeks the wisdom of other authentic, open souls who encourage me to live and love who I am, as I am.
- My true self isn't afraid to admit mistakes or weaknesses or to recognize strengths or gifts.
- My true self sets aside the masks that are put on for the sake of pride, reputation, self-promotion, or self-protection.
- My true self recognizes the sacredness of life itself, looking beyond the temporary, fleeting struggles and embracing with trust all that is held and cherished by God.

Finding and knowing our true self is a never-ending journey that takes time and intention to explore. But in the process, we find deeper freedom to live life with grace as we come to know God and self more deeply.

REST STOP

When have you felt like you weren't being true to yourself? How do you recognize when you may be hiding behind self-made masks? What does it mean for you to "come to what [is your] own?"

2. Emotions or Circumstance

The work of considering the soul identity is not something we do once and check it off the list. Knowing God and knowing self is an every day, every hour, every minute invitation. It's a constant give and take, receiving and releasing, embracing and letting go that occurs as we continually turn our lives toward God. It is recognizing what *doesn't* make up our identity—the roles, titles, accomplishments, and measures of success—and what does.

Our identity is not based on our circumstances. Of course, our location in the time and place of the world impacts and forms our lives in certain ways, and from this pool of experience we offer ourselves to God. These circumstances can and do affect our emotions and our physical body. Trauma or loss can leave us feeling unraveled and defeated, but as Paul writes, "We are afflicted in every way but not crushed, perplexed but not driven to despair . . . . So we do not lose heart. Even though our outer nature is wasting away, our inner being is being renewed day by day" (2 Cor. 4:8, 16). Our changing circumstances never have the last word.

Neither is identity based on emotions driven by our circumstances. Emotions, which are the gift of being human, offer us clues to what may be occurring in our lives, areas where we are struggling, or areas where we are elated. In his book *Into the Silent Land*, Martin Laird uses the metaphor of a mountain and the weather surrounding that mountain to explain our identity being separate from our ever-changing thoughts, moods, and emotions. The weather changes day after day, but the mountain remains. "When we recognize that we *are* Mount Zion,

God's holy dwelling place, and no longer suffer from the illusion that we are the weather, then we are free to let life be as it is at any given moment. We are no longer victims of our afflictive thoughts, but their vigilant witness, silent and free."[5]

Our circumstances and emotions in life can change with the blink of an eye or over the slow passing of time. They play a vital role in the spiritual journey of human existence and how we recognize God in the midst of it all. But beyond our own emotional responses to a set of circumstances, we exist in a still truer identity within the heart of God where we are held secure and can claim our true self as being "wonderfully made" (Ps. 139:14), and "more than victorious" (Rom. 8:37). And when we know this truth in our heart of hearts, then "the truth will make [us] free" (John 8:32).

REST STOP

If you strip it all away, the experiences, emotions, and changing circumstances, what is left at the core? When have you experienced a truth or grace running deeper than the circumstances or traumas you have encountered in life? How did that truth set you free to move beyond the emotions or circumstance?

3. Redefining Roles

At a business gathering years ago, we were asked to introduce ourselves to one another *without* referencing our roles or accomplishments. We all sat silent for a while trying to figure out what we might say. I seem to recall introducing myself at the time as a woman in search of something more. I'm not sure that was my deepest, truest identity, but for a moment it did allow me to step outside the typical connection to job, title, or accomplishment.

While identity does affect the roles we embrace, such roles do not make up the true core of self. That's because our roles change—constantly. Our identity is more than being a parent, a spouse, a CEO or manager, or a friend, as beautiful and God-ordained as those titles may be. Identity derives from the immutable, unchangeable character of God. My identity is woven from the fiber of God's identity. If I truly believe that I am made in the image of God, then I reflect God in my life in some way. Or, as Paul states, "In [God] we live and move and have our being" (Acts 17:28).

To set aside our roles and look deeper within, we can begin by identifying all those roles and examining how we use them to prop ourselves up and to self-proclaim life as meaningful. Of course we love our children, our spouses, our careers, our community connections. But there is so much more beyond our earthly roles that informs who we are at the core of our being. As you spend a few minutes considering what that "so much more" might be for you, consider also how the character of God is woven into your heart and soul. Follow that divine thread and see where it leads you.

REST STOP

Can you define your own soul without the use of a given role? How would you introduce yourself without using any identified role that you currently hold? How does it feel to set aside your roles as a way to get to the heart of your true identity? Is it uncomfortable? Freeing? Or some other response? Write in your journal the words that describe you at the core of your being.

4. Accomplishments and Productivity

It's easy to mistake our accomplishments as part of our identity. After all, these may be memorable markers that help others know us, but they are not our deepest being. I may say "I'm an author," or "I'm a spiritual director," or "I have a degree in . . . ," or I graduated from . . . ," and these may be clues about my passions that lead me deeper into identity. But just like our roles, they only give expression to our truest identity; they are not our identity themselves.

Our cultural insistence on measuring our accomplishments can inflict silent trauma on the soul that we accept as the norm of our existence. From testing and measuring knowledge in schools, to the growth of a church by its number of new members, to key performance indicators in business, to the number of followers on social media, and even to the statistics and rankings of our favorite sports teams, we are never far from the world's demand that we be identified by the measurement of our life activity.

Of course measurement has its purpose and can help keep us on track to meet goals. But it often goes beyond that purpose. It becomes our pastime, our obsession, and it often controls how we feel about ourselves. Meanwhile, the only metric I can find in scripture is offered by John the Baptist in relationship to knowing Jesus when he said, "He must increase, but I must decrease" (John 3:30).

This is paradox. For if I decrease it seems I might lose myself entirely. But in reality it brings me closer to my true self. This decreasing of self occurs when we strip away the false identities of our roles, titles, accomplishments, and measures of success. The writer of Hebrews says that before God "no creature is hidden, but all are naked and laid bare" (4:13). We are seen and fully known and loved in the eyes of the Creator. As we set aside all that is not needed, the soul does not diminish but rather expands into a spacious place, throwing open windows into the soul and doorways into divine presence. In self-relinquishment we find freedom and finally a sense of comfort and completeness within our own skin.

REST STOP

This week, take note of all the ways that you live by the numbers rather than by the Spirit. What is your relationship to your "metrics of success"? Contemplate what your life is all about without the measurements and indicators of success or growth. How might you loosen your grip on yourself just a bit to let your soul soar?

5. Knowing God, Knowing Self

As we've set aside those false identities that we rely on to prop up our sense of worth—our roles, titles, accomplishments, emotions, and circumstances—we have yet another step to take. We've cast off the old ways of thinking about our activity and measurements of success. This frees us then to turn our attention to what we find as the foundation of our identity.

This action of casting off the old and putting on the new is the first exercise in exploring identity. "You have stripped off the old self with its practices and have clothed yourselves with the new self, which is being renewed in knowledge according to the image of its creator" (Col. 3:9-10). This isn't always easy to do because our self-talk is often the last outpost of resistance before delving into the essence of our true self. We're hard on ourselves. We don't like to give ourselves a break or offer tenderness to our wounded selves. But the clue to our deepest identity lies within the image of the Creator, the *imago dei.*

We typically think of being "made in God's image" as being given divine attributes instilled in all humanity and lived out in vast expressions and dimensions. Because we are "like God" we reflect that Divine image. We are creative because God is creative. We love because God is love. We are relational because God is relational through the expression of Father, Son, and Holy Spirit. But there is more. At a deeper place of knowing, being made in the Divine image calls for seeking out the essence of life that God *imagines* for each of us individually and communally.

What we call being-made-in-God's-image is the result of the Divine imagination that created all that is, seen and unseen, not just for the purpose of stockpiling divine works of art but to weave it all into one interconnected, regenerative network of belonging, where every unique and singular being plays a part and is interdependent on the other. How we define or recognize our God-imagined self will open to us in unique ways, sometimes in "aha" moments, mostly in the slow process and work of God where we are invited to participate in that Divine nature through our own believing, faith-forward imaginations. Regardless of what our self-talk may tell us, scripture confirms we are God's *handiwork* (Eph. 2:10, NIV), derived from the Greek word *poiema*, the root of our English word *poem*. We each live a God-given life intended as poetic expression of the Divine imagination.

This is how God imagines us to be as our truest selves. Our job is to listen for and live out that poetic life as we give ourselves over to the creative and transformative power of the Divine Presence at work in the studio of our souls.

REST STOP

Spend time this week building your awareness of the self-talk habits that affect your attitudes particularly when a day has felt challenging. As you consider these habits of the heart, ask God to help you strip away the old to renew your knowledge "according to the image of its creator." Can you take the pages of your life and capture in poetic terms what life has been like for you thus far or in this season? Just a few descriptive words strung together become a poetic expression that says, "This is who I am." Dig deeper and look beneath the mere circumstance or emotional state, and see if you can identify the strength of your heart in these difficult times.

6. The Voice of Silence

Sometimes silence makes the loudest statement. The voice of silence insists that what exists in that stillness deserves to be recognized for what it is. As Jesus stands silent in the midst of his accusers, even Pilate can hear what the silence is saying. Pilate asks, "'Do you not hear how many accusations they make against you?' But [Jesus] gave him no answer, not even to a single charge, so that the governor was greatly amazed" (Matt. 27:13-14).

Amid the activity and confusion, the inquiry and the furious pace to accomplish their mission of doing away with him, Jesus remains a calm center in the eye of the storm. Visibly undisturbed by false accusations, by demands for answers, by physical abuse to bend the will, Jesus remains still. On occasion he responds but always in truth and with the assurance and focus on God's will.

There was no need to answer. He had no need or intention to negotiate his identity based on the opinions of others. His life had been his testimony; the people who walked about Israel healed, free, or somehow changed bore witness to his faithful acts of love. It was too late for words to matter now. Truth would only inflame the Pharisees' thirst for blood. In the silence, they stood with their accusations in hand, shouldering the weight of their own words, the weight of their lies, while Jesus remained silent—confidently silent—in his own identity.

Often our lives cry out to Jesus for answers. Most of our biggest questions start with "why?" *Why don't you take this burden from me? Why do I have to suffer because of someone else's mistakes? Why did she have to die? Why can't he be healed? Why do wars rage? Why don't you do something?* And we demand answers but mostly come up against silence. Yet in this stillness we recognize that God alone is sovereign and worthy of worship. And we realize the question is not so much *why*, but rather *who*? And we enter the divine mystery that is the silence of God reflected in the silence of the Christ.

REST STOP

When have you encountered silence that seems to have made a grand or profound statement without words? What kind of events or observations have left you speechless? How can those moments of silence become prayer?

7. Soul Talk

For personal reflection, spiritual direction dialogue, small group discussion, or on retreat

Lectio Divina: Psalm 51

Slowly and prayerfully read aloud Psalm 51, and listen for the voice of God. Listen for a word or phrase that resonates or catches the attention of your heart. Hold that word or phrase within you during a minute of silence. Now, slowly read the verses again, listening for deeper connection, invitation, or guidance related to the word or phrase. What is God saying to you through this scripture passage in this time and place?

After another period of silence, journal what you've received, heard, or longed for. If you're with a group, briefly share the word and your reflection from this reading with one another, listening without comment or the need to give advice or even agreement. Simply hold the divine words received in safe and welcoming silence.

The Inner Path of Identity

- If you journaled through each of the six readings, go back and review your journal entries. What thread connects your thoughts? What is the prevalent theme of your reflections? How might that thread be woven into a prayer?

- If you haven't journaled, simply reflect on the readings. What has stuck with you? What rises as important for your own journey? What words or thoughts did you underline?
- What have you most frequently relied upon to identify yourself in the past? Your accomplishments, roles, emotions, or some other factor?
- What aspects of your life or attitudes feel like they need to be cast off or released to expand and receive something new from the Spirit at work within you?
- What does comprise your identity? Give words to who you are.

Receiving Grace

What grace or gift do you most desire from God as you consider the inner path of identity as a doorway for drawing closer to the Divine?

THE PATH OF

COMMUNITY

"Our soul waits for the LORD;
he is our help and shield.
Our heart is glad in him
because we trust in his holy name.
Let your steadfast love, O LORD, be upon us,
even as we hope in you."

PSALM 33:20-22

Most of our soul talk is listening to our own heart. But Psalm 33 suggests that we also collectively share a soul with "all the inhabitants of the earth" (v. 14) and share particularly with "those who hope in his steadfast love" (v. 18). What is it about belonging to others in community that makes life feel fuller, richer, safer, and more complete? And at the same time, what is it about community that can make life feel more challenging?

In community, soul speaks to soul. We recognize our own pain when we see others who are suffering in some way. And we recognize our own joys when we share the joy of others.

Community—this is our word for a "common unity." It's easy to lose sight of what unites us when there are battles being waged over policy, preferences, and power. Yet in community we learn grace—both how to receive it and how to give it. And in this unity of grace, we find God whose "work is done in faithfulness. . . . the earth is full of the steadfast love of the LORD" (vv. 4-5).

Even as we give and receive grace we bless one another, and *our* heart and soul is glad as God's steadfast love falls upon us.

1. Support Systems

Since the beginning of time, humans have needed one another's support. "It is not good that [people] should be alone," God declares at Creation (Gen. 2:18). We all have experienced the pain of loneliness, separation, or isolation. But just as a vine searches out the support of a tree, a wall, or a trellis to give it direction and stability, so too our lives reach further, find connection, and thrive within a healthy support system.

We may or may not have been born into a family that supports us. As we grow and launch out on our own, we define our own support system beyond our family. I recognize my own support structure in my family, in a few close friendships, in work relationships, in a faith community, and even in those whose words support me from ages past.

The need for support may be the reason why I love my work as a spiritual director. Spiritual direction[6], also called spiritual companioning, is a practice that calls me to intentionally partner with others on this journey through life. The majority of my work is in actively listening to the one I companion, and this active listening is a gift I both give and receive. It allows us to tend the holy amid daily life. It pushes us to search out and recognize God's presence in all things, inviting us always to lean into the grace of the Divine. When we find those connection points with others in community, we see God more fully, both within ourselves and within others.

We can try to do life on our own, but oh, the benefits we reap in community with others. Community allows us to show up to explore our own lives, to know the Divine within, and to respond to the call to belong with others. Living in community is living fully as we're created to be.

REST STOP

How have you built your own support system? Who does it include? Which areas of your life feel like they need more support? Where might you reach out to find that support? Where are the safe places, the listening spaces where you feel heard and seen as you are, where you are? If you don't have such a place, consider creating one. Read more about the possibility in appendix 1.

2. Reimagining Church

Church as we know it is being recreated. Does that feel scary, dangerous, risky? Or inviting, hopeful, and exciting? Or maybe we can agree that it is all those things. Blame it on the pandemic, politics, or cultural and generational shifts: The church, and nearly every individual connected to it, is rethinking and reimagining what it means to be "the body of Christ." Some call this "deconstructing faith," but I prefer to think of it as reimagining faith. Reimagining the church and the congregation is opening doors to new ways of expressing our journey together.

Most people—churchgoers and otherwise—are noticing that these shifts have brought us into ourselves. We are discerning what is important to the spiritual life—what is life-giving and how we can experience a deeper intimacy with the Divine while learning to be present to ourselves and others. This kind of inner reflection cries for an expression of faith that is outside the realm of what has typically been offered within the church. Yet equipping the church to help people on this journey inward is what Paul prays for his church in Ephesus, so that they "may be strengthened in [their] inner being" (Eph. 3:16).

How can the church minister to individuals exploring their faith, longing to know the presence of God in their ordinary lives? The possibilities are unlimited, but perhaps those possibilities can be gathered under one umbrella called "listening." The traditions of the church focus on teaching, telling, speaking, preaching, discipling. But few are set up with people trained simply to listen, to see people where they are, to be a companion, to be a presence with others on their journey.

What a difference it might make for those wrestling with their faith to find grace and hospitality within the church that welcomes them into a conversation that allows them to be heard. What a unique gift to offer to individuals living in a noisy world. In a listening and companioning posture, we bring no agenda to "fix their faith" but to simply be with them, to listen, to see, and to bear witness to their journey as holy ground.

I know, it's scary—and exciting and hope-filled. Reimagining what it means to be the church is the co-creative work of the Spirit, calling us to draw closer to the Divine One, to open the doors a little wider to a broader expression of what it means to walk with Jesus through this life.

REST STOP

How has your experience of church or a faith community changed over the past few years? What faith community listens to your story and journey in a safe environment? How might you build that support group if one doesn't exist? What difference might it make to share your journey more intentionally with a spiritual director or friend?

3. The Power of Liturgy

Whenever I visit my ninety-two-year-old mother, I recognize further decline of her memory, her loss of vocabulary, the frailty of her gait, and her diminishing eyesight. But I also recognize the increased importance of her daily liturgy, her desire for community, and her commitment to her faith. *Liturgy* is a term often used in the context of the church and the rituals we enact as symbolic reminders of our faith. But liturgy is practiced much more broadly by each individual in the ordinary moments of life. These rituals help us to embody our faith, to live out in bodily form what we believe and hold dear to our hearts. Liturgy isn't intended to keep us tied to a particular habit but rather invites us to a divine feast, a table set before us amid our daily life and challenges.

Morning liturgy for my mother begins with coffee and toast and reading her Bible. It has been the same for as long as I can remember. I marvel at the sacredness of this ordinary, life-giving routine. For here is the bread. And here is the cup. And she receives the Living Word as true sustenance for her soul.

Her liturgy has filled me as well. It lives on in my own very similar morning liturgy. My daughter recently told me that her morning unfolds in much the same way. A legacy of quiet morning pause, honoring the beginning of a new day. Prayers offered and journals filled as we recognize the power of liturgy to ground us in our day allowing the Divine to hallow our activity.

The same beauty of liturgy is much of the reason why church remains life-giving to me. Regardless of the human weaknesses we bring into the faith community, the friction we may experience, the disappointment in programs or people, there remains a steadying core of liturgy that ministers to the body of Christ. Even in the simplest, most casual, small church gathering, there is a rhythm to the time together. We likely are welcomed as we enter, a candle may be lit, we sit before a space designated as the altar. We sing, we pray, we hear the Word read and preached. We present our offerings. We are blessed as we "pass the peace" to one another in greeting. And we leave with the blessing of benediction.

Somehow, despite the crying baby in the back row, the ringing cell phone that someone forgot to turn off during the service, or even the mediocre singing, liturgy realigns my heart to God. It asks that I look beyond my daily routines and even my own personal liturgy and enter into the mystery of the Divine Presence with others around me. For an hour or so, I set aside the stresses, the work that awaits my return, the chores that always need to be completed, and I enter the holy liturgy of prayer and praise as I come to the altar. For here is the bread. And here is the cup. And I marvel at the sacredness of this life-giving liturgy sustaining my soul.

REST STOP

What part of your daily routine feels like liturgy in your life? If it's difficult to recognize it as an invitation to the holy, how might you incorporate a sacred pause to be present to the divine invitations? In your faith community, what does your typical liturgy look like? What part of the liturgy speaks to you and sustains you in some way? How can you offer yourself more fully to God during your church service or set-aside time?

4. Call to Community

As churches come to reimagine what it means to be the church in today's world, we find glimmers of direction in reading about the first church established after Jesus' ascension into heaven. Acts 2 tells us that this church was "devoted," filled with "awe . . . and had all things in common" (vv. 42-44). I honestly can't claim that my church experiences over the years have felt like this. The words I might use would be *curious, filled with questions, searching for unity*. But if we consider these characteristics of the early church, we can find guidance in the rebirth of our church communities.

Devoted. Being devoted to a faith community feels a little old-fashioned. But the scripture is specific about being devoted to teaching and fellowship. If I'm devoted to the teachings of Jesus, then I'm listening and attentive to what God is saying to me. And since the writer of Acts connects being devoted to the teachings to also being devoted to fellowship, this is reason to connect with others in sharing what we hear and what we are learning on the faith journey.

Filled with awe. I sense this is something more than feeling inspired or lifted up by a message or a song. It isn't an emotion but a gift given by God. Some translations say that "awe came upon them." Awe invokes a humbling of the heart and the spirit to recognize and receive the divine message. Some days I "feel" worshipful and humbled, other days I don't. But the closest I've come to experiencing this sense of awe was in a church that routinely called the congregation into a space of silence before receiving the teaching of the morning. Not silence with background "mood" music—just plain silence that strips you bare of self-conscious thoughts or pretense. Together we took a collective deep breath and became conscious of the holy in a communal posture of openness and expectancy.

Everything in common. I've come to believe that there is really only one thing we truly have in common, and that is the holy ground at the foot of the cross of Christ. It is central to everything, the literal "crux" of the matter. The cross unites us and defines us. Regardless of how "uncommon" or out of place one may feel in the faith community, this *one* thing—the cross—is *everything.* And so we can truly say we share *everything* in common.

Jesus comes to the world to unite us. His wounds wash and heal us. His resurrection anoints us with the salve of peace. Our soul maladies are not fatal injuries. Our dis-eased lives are not terminal afflictions. Together, in common unity, we are being transformed.

REST STOP

Read through Acts 2, which describes the life of the first church. Which of these attributes can you relate to your own community life? What areas are a mystery or challenge to you? What areas would you like to explore further? This week experiment with creating a regular time for silence in your daily life, particularly as you enter into worship with others. How can silence unite a group?

5. Bear with One Another

I have a friend who has belonged to a church for decades. She recently told me that she feels a "benign neglect" to her presence in the congregation. Spoken to, yes. Acknowledged as present, yes. But not truly embraced. It's a pain point for her now, and she wonders what it all means and where it will take her.

Living in community doesn't always lead to a spiritual high. In fact, as much as I believe we are called to live out our faith in community, I also realize it is often the most difficult place to be. To be honest, it would be easy to walk away from community at times, like when I feel lonely in the midst of a gathering, or when I'm hurt by being misunderstood, or I feel like I need to explain myself to be accepted.

The challenges of community life are endless. Surely there is no perfect community. There is no community that exists solely to meet my specific needs and to operate according to my preferences. This is why we are reminded to conduct ourselves "with patience, bearing with one another in love" (Eph. 4:2). We don't need to "bear with one another" when things are going smoothly. It's when someone is stepping on my last nerve that I need to practice patience and bear with that person in love. We all react to circumstances and people in ways that may be grace-less. I know because I've been that person.

Yet I cannot deny that community is the very essence of the Divine expressed as Creator, Son, and Spirit dwelling together in unity. I see Jesus living day in and day out with a small band of followers who certainly tried his patience with their lack of faith, their fears, their positioning for power, their lack of understanding. Yet he bore with them in love. He saw beyond the rough façades and the failures. He saw their hidden desires that they themselves could not yet name. And he invited them to draw closer, to know God more deeply, and to be loved by God. Community was never an option or a choice for Jesus. It was and is simply who he is, part of his being. And he invites us to live in community in this world.

REST STOP

How would you describe your own relationship with your faith community (whether that is a traditional church or a small group of faithful friends who know you and encourage you)? How would you describe your faith community's relationship to you? In what ways are you growing in patience and the ability to bear with one another in love? What are the obstacles to this growth? What is the line between bearing with others or feeling abused by a community in some way? When do you know it is time to find a new community?

6. The Road to Calvary

From Gethsemane to the governor's palace, now on to Golgotha. Jesus reaches exhaustion and already draws near to death. He likely hasn't slept in twenty-four hours. It's doubtful his need for food or water has been considered let alone attended to. Dehydrated, wounded, bruised, and bleeding, he attempts to drag the cross placed over his torn back and shoulders. But the pace is unbearably slow. How every nerve of his body must cry out to stop the pain, and at the same time we have to wonder if the thought of death might seem a relief for him.

Somehow, he finds the courage and fortitude to go on, to take another step closer to his death on that cross. And as he does, we draw closer to God, closer to the Holy of Holies, closer to the hope of our souls. Scripture tells us that multitudes of people follow, facing the cross (see Luke 23:27). A diverse community, bound together by this event, takes its place in the scene. Those who love Jesus walk right alongside his enemies. Some are at the height of their religious experience; some simply stumble upon Jesus, like an interruption to their lives; some find him in the midst of their mourning; some are on their way to do business or meet family.

Regardless of circumstance or status in life, we all, at one time or another, face the cross. We encounter Jesus in passing or as we've sought him out and sat at his feet. But we all come and encounter the suffering Savior, the wounded Lamb of God, and there we respond. Do we follow or forget? Do we worship or weep? Do we join him on the long journey or continue on our own way?

REST STOP

As you meditate on the scene of watching Jesus travel this road and bear his cross, what do you see? Where might you place yourself in this picture? Close enough to reach out and touch Jesus or hidden in the crowd? Offering words of encouragement, weeping, silently praying? Are there others in the crowd you recognize or want to travel with as you make your way to the crucifixion site? Record your prayer of imagination in your journal.

7. Soul Talk

For personal reflection, spiritual direction dialogue, small group discussion, or on retreat

Lectio Divina: Psalm 33

Slowly and prayerfully read aloud Psalm 33 and listen for the voice of God. Listen for a word or phrase that resonates or catches the attention of your heart. Hold that word or phrase within you during a minute of silence. Now, slowly read the verses again, listening for deeper connection, invitation, or guidance related to the word or phrase. What is God saying to you through this scripture passage in this time and place?

After another period of silence, journal what you've received, heard, or longed for. If you're with a group, briefly share the word and your reflection from this reading with one another, listening without comment or the need to give advice or even agreement. Simply hold the divine words received in safe and welcoming silence.

The Inner Path of Community

- If you journaled through each of the six readings, go back and review your journal entries. What thread connects your thoughts? What is the prevalent theme of your reflections? How might that thread be woven into a prayer?

- If you haven't journaled, simply reflect on the readings. What has stuck with you? What rises as important for your own journey? What words or thoughts did you underline?
- How would you describe the gift of community?
- How would you describe the challenge of community?

Receiving Grace

What grace or gift do you most desire from God as you consider the inner path of community as a doorway for drawing closer to the Divine?

THE PATH OF
CONTEMPLATION

But I have calmed and quieted my soul,
like a weaned child with its mother;
my soul is like the weaned child that is with me.

Psalm 131:2

There comes a time when the soul outgrows the need to grab for nourishment or answers or formulas for spiritual growth. Whatever we find on our path through life, we welcome it all as opportunity to intimately know God. Our hard labor to serve, to make things happen, to control outcomes, and to measure our growth is gone as we break through to a place where we find rest for the soul.

Life becomes anchored in the present moment where contentment reigns, and we abandon ourselves to divine providence, knowing that regardless of hardships or needs, turmoil or conflict, nothing separates us from God because nothing is separate from God.

In a silent, contemplative unity, rest in the endless and lavish love of God as a child quieted within the mother's embrace.

1. Ebb and Flow

The contemplative life takes us deeper into life with God, but there is always an ebbing and flowing force at work, a natural inward and outward rhythm of knowing God associated with our willingness to yield ourselves to divine grace and truth. Our cultural tendency—and sometimes the tendency of the church—is to quickly pull people outward into "active duty" before they have fully explored what it means to know God and to recognize God's voice and call. Invariably, this random activity labeled as "service" does not provide the spiritual nourishment we seek. We wonder if this is all there is to the spiritual life. Can we truly know and be known by God through an overactive schedule? The book of James says that faith without action is dead (see 2:26). And the opposite is also true: Works without a living faith is dead.

We must journey inward, slowing down to explore our own stories, ask questions, find our "truth in the inward being," as David says in Psalm 51:6. As we uncover that truth and find God loving us in the midst of it all, we then feel the nudge outward again into the greater world. But this time we are informed by the Spirit, where the love of God changes our perspectives.

Over and over again we make this journey in and out. The metaphor of the ocean moving in and out provides some options for visualizing this ebb and flow, and interpretation provides choices as to who or what is ebbing or flowing. At times we may feel that God is the ocean, flowing over us and then ebbing away to reveal hidden bits of life for our contemplation. Other times we see ourselves as the ocean waves, crashing outward toward the world and then returning to the encompassing presence of God.

We are connected to the divine force that moves within us, calling us in and calling us out until we realize that movement in and movement out really are one and the same thing. Just as the ocean is not distinctly separate from land, so too we experience a coexistent union with God in the forming, reforming, and transforming wonder of life.

REST STOP

How and when have you experienced a sense of ebb and flow in your spiritual life? What areas of your life feel like it's ebbing or flowing today? Is this a rhythm that you fight against to avoid the up-and-down, the in-and-out of a situation? What treasures have you discovered about your life as you experience ebb and flow?

2. A Spacious Place

Most of us live what we call "ordinary lives," and regardless of our perceptions of what would be more exciting, every life feels ordinary to the person living it. Even if I am, for instance, a celebrated concert pianist traveling the world with symphonic orchestras, what I do as a pianist is my ordinary life that involves hours of practice, rehearsals, endless flights, living out of a suitcase, working at night, and getting my concert attire sent to the dry cleaners. Ordinary living can begin to feel stifling, narrow, and dull if we aren't open to the underlying truth that every breath we breathe is a holy, God-given gift in which we have the potential to enter into the intimate, sacred dwelling place of the soul.

In this dwelling place we may begin by recognizing our own condition—physically, emotionally, intellectually, or spiritually. Imagine these threads of life being integrated into one cohesive life of beauty. We offer these threads to God, the great soul-weaver, who receives each one as gift. My threads on this given day include weariness, both physical and emotional. And here is a thread of disappointment that runs through my work life, feeling like I'm not measuring up in some way. A thread of boredom, maybe discontentment that I'm lost in a life of performing minor tasks and chores that all together don't measure up to what I would call satisfaction or meaning.

But once these threads are given over to God, I am free to relax, to stop fretting and ruminating as I let the master-artist design my life. I no longer need to see the big picture results of my life and what I've accomplished as I receive the grace to simply trust God's good work in me at this time and place. I may feel weary, but I am invited to trust that

God will ultimately restore my strength or fill in the gaps and redeem my time and energy through other means.

Along with the thread of disappointment or not "measuring up," the Spirit also asks that I turn over the measuring stick I've used to come to this self-deprecating conclusion. And I see the measuring rod snapped in two and tossed aside as I realize my life is not measured by outcomes but by the value of simply being alive on this day, on any day, to experience the gift of breathing, dreaming, doing, learning, touching, and being renewed in body, mind, and spirit.

I can say, indeed, along with the psalmists, "The boundary lines have fallen for me in pleasant places" (Ps. 16:6); and "We went through fire and through water; yet you have brought us out to a spacious place" (Ps. 66:12). The eternal, immortal, infinite, all-wise God comes to us, meets us, invites us to leave behind our limiting ideas and claustrophobic perceptions of life. In faith we recognize that even in the ordinary tasks of daily living, we are at home in the spacious place of lavish love and divine grace.

REST STOP

In what ways has your life felt limiting or constricted? What impact has that had on you physically, emotionally, or in your relationships? What symbol might you bring into the presence of God to represent the things that keep you living in the narrow space? As you come to God with these things and enter a spacious and pleasant place, how does your situation or your attitude shift or change?

3. An Integrated Life

Living an integrated life has been an important topic for me personally for years. In fact, a sense of *dis-integration* was one of the reasons I first started meeting with a spiritual director years ago. I felt like I was living a work life, a family life, a church life, and probably a few other lives. But it all felt disjointed, separate, apart from one another. It left me wondering which was the most authentic me.

I think the kitchen is the best place to study integration, which is interesting considering that I am "kitchen resistant." I've never had a love for cooking, baking, and especially the cleaning that goes along with it. But I'm coming into my own in planning, prepping, and executing a great recipe or meal.

I am finding that the kitchen is a perfect place to meditate, opening a deeper awareness to the gifts of the senses—the texture of dough, the aroma of roasting meat, the sweetness of a deep-red strawberry, the sounds of the sizzle, the boil, the slicing and dicing. I'm also mindful that I may have all the ingredients necessary for a great recipe, but if I don't *integrate* all those ingredients together, it may drastically change the look and taste of the dish.

And so it is with the soul. If we fail to contemplate and sit with those parts of life that have been left unattended and unwelcomed into the whole, we miss out on the possibility of those parts and pieces becoming something greater than the sum of their parts. Those orphaned parts invariably develop a life of their own and cry out to be reclaimed as beloved. Learning to integrate all of life—darkness and light, sorrow and celebration—takes time and attention.

So how does one tend to those parts and pieces to bring life into its wholeness? A good place to start is in a notebook or journal. A regular habit of awareness, reflection, capturing memories, thoughts, and dreams has proven to be part of the healing path for many. It's a way to give voice to what has been silenced for so long. Another practice is to take an inventory of memories and events year by year through your life. A list of these captured moments throughout the years will give you a picture of the highs and lows, and the memories that evoke the most emotion or response are ones that you may want to explore more deeply in writing or with a trusted friend or counselor. Finally, the practice of a daily or weekly prayer of Examen intentionally offers up life to God, asking as the psalmist did to "Search me, O God, and know my heart; test me and know my thoughts" (139:23).

When we take the time, we can arrive at healing and wholeness that allows us to savor the good and abundant life that welcomes all, that meets us on the path of knowing God and knowing ourselves.

REST STOP

What parts of your life feel like they've been left out of the whole—an unfulfilled dream, an absent parent or life partner, your childhood, a family secret? How might you find ways (through conversation or action) to welcome that part of your life that has been sitting outside of your own soul? How have those forgotten parts played a role in making you who you are today?

4. Measuring Fullness

This past year I've meditated on the prayer that Paul penned in his letter to the Ephesian church: "I pray that you may have the power to comprehend, with all the saints, what is the breadth and length and height and depth and to know the love of Christ that surpasses knowledge, so that you may be filled with all the fullness of God" (3:18-19). I'm awed by this prayer and by the possibility of being filled with God's fullness. That single word—*fullness*—has begun to arise as a two-syllable centering prayer throughout my day. I'm exploring new images of what God has in mind for me when I pray this passage.

At the same time, it seems incomprehensible to me that we can be filled with the fullness of an eternal, all-knowing God who has no limits and no beginning or ending. While God's fullness exists beyond any earthly dimension, the reference to breadth, length, height, and depth implies a *measurable* fullness in *human* terms. And this reminds me that I don't need to see or comprehend to the edge of eternity to understand the fullness of God. Maybe I simply need to consider my human capacity that does have its limits.

Consider a small bucket immersed in the ocean as a picture of a life fully filled with the fullness of God. The bucket is filled to its full capacity of the ocean, yet it does not contain the entirety of the ocean. Even if that bucket is riddled with imperfections, it is still fully immersed, covered, and filled with the ocean flowing through those imperfections. So it is with our imperfect lives. We have the capacity to receive and know the fullness of God completing us, immersing us, covering us, moving through us in every dimension of our lives. And in this I have full access to "the peace of God, which surpasses [my] understanding" about any given situation (Phil. 4:7). And I will know the love of Christ that surpasses my knowledge (see Eph. 3:19). And I will receive love that overflows "more and more with knowledge and full insight" even when my own ability to love feels depleted (Phil. 1:9). This is the fullness of God.

We need not struggle to know the immensity of God. Here within the constraints of our own common life, we touch the edgeless, limitless, eternal, infinite reality of God ever and always filling us with the full measure of divine love.

REST STOP

Spend some time meditating on how it feels to know God's love filling you and flowing through every dimension of your life. What difference might it make to consider this fullness as a way to pray through your daily life, imagining it flowing in and through your experiences, your pain points, your victories? Experiment with this kind of prayer of imagination this week and see what impact it has on your relationship with God.

5. An Earthy Holiness

The painting by Jean-Francois Millet entitled *The Angelus* depicts two peasants praying in a field, a small basket of potatoes between them. On the horizon is a distant church. The title and composition implies that the two are giving thanks for their small harvest at the end of the workday as the church bell rings. This image speaks to me for a couple of reasons.

First, it reminds me that as much time as I spend seeking the contemplative life through prayer, there is always an invitation to stay grounded in the very earthbound elements of being human. This is the literal ground of our being and the place where God dwells within our daily work and rituals of staying alive.

Second, it reminds me of my move from the busy metropolis of Phoenix, Arizona, to the tiny port town of Port Orchard in the Pacific Northwest. The first Sunday that I attended church in Port Orchard, the congregation was celebrating a church-wide potato harvest. They had brought pounds and pounds of brown, bulgy, homegrown potatoes into the church in baskets, bags, and boxes to be donated to a local food bank. The pastor offered a blessing of the potatoes, and the potluck following the worship service served, of course, potato dishes.

It reminded me of how grounded our contemplative lives must be in the simple human experiences of life. Jesus taught us this lesson when he said, "Look at the birds of the air" and "the lilies of the field" (Matt. 6:26, 28) He made sacred a simple meal of bread and wine and so calls us to consider the everyday affairs of this earth as holy ground.

I love that all the world can be offered up as prayer, as a doorway into thanks, praise, lament, or blessing. It helps to remember that life itself is prayer, where I can bless a potato, or stand in awe of a roly-poly potato bug, and praise the Giver of every good and perfect gift. For here in such earthbound realities God dwells with us.

REST STOP

How is God's grand creation in our world impacting you these days? How might you bless the God-given gifts of creation with gratitude? When was the last time that the earth brought you to a place of awe or an epiphany moment? If you can't recall such a time, schedule a day to spend outside hiking, resting on a beach or lakeside, or planting flowers in a pot, a yard, or offering to do so for a neighbor or organization. As you do, be on the lookout for how God is speaking to you in the natural environment, then record that earthy interaction in your journal.

6. The Pathway Home

The Gospels reveal Jesus living in contemplative community. The story of the two disciples walking home to Emmaus late in the day following the news of Jesus' resurrection is one of the most revealing stories of Jesus' contemplative life. We see how Jesus attends to their journey. We understand the tenderness involved as he allows their story to unfold naturally. He doesn't rush in and reveal the truth of the resurrection. He walks by their side and stays with them as they discover it for themselves.

Of course, Jesus knows what is on their minds. He knows how they are feeling and where they are going, yet he doesn't intrude on their journey. He supports their process of examining all that has made them sad as a result of the crucifixion events. He helps them explore their confusion about what had happened to Jesus that morning. Jesus simply asks questions, listens, stays with them, and lets them experience the sadness until the moment when it can all be made clear to them.

We often desire easy explanations about our faith. We want solutions to challenges, fixes to brokenness, and clear maps to get us on the path to happiness. But Jesus doesn't offer any of that. What he does offer is presence. He comes near. He goes with them. He listens to them as they are on that path.

We too can take on this demeanor as we encounter others on their journey of faith. Whether within our faith communities or out in our daily lives, we can offer the same gifts of presence and listening, which are rare in this world. As Christ followers, this is how we are called to be the hands and feet of Christ—to be a listening presence to others, to bear with one another, to mourn with those who mourn, to rejoice with those who rejoice. When we come to the resurrection journey willing to explore our own experiences and ready to listen as others do the same, we see that Jesus was with us all along.

REST STOP

Consider how Jesus has met you on the road and listened and revealed truth and wisdom in your life. What next step are you being invited to on your faith journey? When have you experienced sadness, disappointment, or discouragement on your spiritual journey? How were you aware of Jesus meeting you in this time? How have you felt listened to and heard during difficult times? How have you been a listening presence to others? What difference might it make to you or your faith community to have such a posture of listening deeply to one another?

7. Soul Talk

For personal reflection, spiritual direction dialogue, small group discussion, or on retreat

Lectio Divina: Psalm 131

Slowly and prayerfully read aloud Psalm 131 describing a contemplative soul. Listen for a word or phrase that resonates or catches the attention of your heart. Hold that word or phrase within you during a minute of silence. Now, slowly read the verses again, listening for deeper connection, invitation, or guidance related to the word or phrase. What is God saying to you through this scripture passage in this time and place?

After another period of silence, journal what you've received, heard, or longed for. If you're with a group, briefly share the word and your reflection from this reading with one another, listening without comment or the need to give advice or even agreement. Simply hold the divine words received in safe and welcoming silence.

The Path of Contemplation

- If you journaled through each of the six readings, go back and review your journal entries. What thread connects your thoughts? What is the prevalent theme of your reflections? How might that thread be woven into a prayer?

- If you haven't journaled, simply reflect on the readings. What has stuck with you? What rises as important for your own journey? What words or thoughts did you underline?
- Where were you challenged with the idea of contemplation?
- What would it mean to you if your life included a slower pace and moments for stillness, reflection, and prayer?
- What invitation are you sensing related to the contemplative path?
- What do you need to release or change to make room for attending to that invitation?

Receiving Grace

What grace or gift do you most desire from God as you consider the invitation to a more contemplative life as a doorway for drawing closer to the Divine?

EPILOGUE

Through sacred paths, we have explored the sound of the soul speaking as well as the voice of God within. And while most don't experience God's voice in exacting words and human tones, the soul has capacity to recognize the invitations, the subtle movements, the moments of awakening, and the deepening desire for the Divine amid all that life throws our way.

This is a journey that has no end. We won't fully arrive at the destination in this life. Always we are beginning. Always we are on a pilgrimage through this earthly existence. And always we are in the company of others who travel the sacred inner journey. Together we listen to the soul speak.

> "*For God alone my soul waits in silence, for my hope is from him*" (Ps. 62:5).
>
> "*O God, you are my God; I seek you; my soul thirsts for you; my flesh faints for you, as in a dry and weary land where there is no water*" (Ps. 63:1).
>
> "*My soul longs, indeed it faints, for the courts of the* Lord; *my heart and my flesh sing for joy to the living God*" (Ps. 84:2).
>
> "*My soul refuses to be comforted. I think of God, and I moan; I meditate, and my spirit faints*" (Ps. 77:2-3).

"You desire truth in the inward being; therefore teach me wisdom in my secret heart" (Ps. 51:6).

"Our soul waits for the L*ORD . . . our help and shield"* (Ps. 33:20).

"I have calmed and quieted my soul, like a weaned child with its mother; my soul is like the weaned child that is with me" (Ps. 131:2).

May your soul be free of all that is not needed.

May it be open to all that is being given.

May you walk the path that leads you home to the divine center of your truest self.

May you know the intimate presence of Jesus always walking with you as you listen to God speaking into your life.

APPENDIX 1
LEADER'S GUIDE

Active listening is becoming a lost art in our world, including in our faith communities. It is a rare gift to offer a safe place for others to share their journey without judgment or interference. After reading through *Speak, My Soul*, you may be wondering how you can encourage others to listen for the Divine with holy purpose. This leader's guide will help you discern if leading a listening group is the next step for you and, if so, how to go about it. It offers instruction and insight into group dynamics in general, specific insight into each week's sacred path, and suggestions for engaging as a group around each week's topic.

Defining the Listening Group: Since the group format of a listening group is much different than a traditional book club or study group, it does require some thought and intention to making it the safe and welcoming place where others can explore their own spiritual journey. Define this group and its goals before you begin inviting others to join. Use the following information to summarize the text and outline the benefits of a *Speak, My Soul* group.

> *Speak, My Soul* is a roadmap for exploring the landscape of the soul, identifying seven sacred paths on the spiritual journey. These include the following:
>
> - The Path of Discernment
> - The Path of Discipline

- The Path of Abiding
- The Path in the Wilderness
- The Path of Identity
- The Path of Community
- The Path of Contemplation

Each pathway leads to conversations of the heart through daily personal reflection, journaling, and devotional prayer. You're invited to share in community as we learn to settle into our own souls, reflect on our experiences, trust our own journey, and recognize the movement of the Spirit amid daily life.

Speak, My Soul will offer the following benefits to the group:

- A roadmap for walking the path toward a deeper connection to God, to self, and to others
- A rhythm for personal devotion and a means of sharing that journey with others
- Guided reflections at the end of each reading to respond to as prayerful dialogue with God through journaling
- A weekly gathering with the group to actively listen to one another as we explore and discover our own inner pathway

Forming a Group: Once you've decided to form a group, the best approach is to personally invite individuals to be part of the group rather than making it an open call to everyone in a larger community. If there is greater interest from a large group of persons, consider teaming up with other individuals to offer multiple smaller groups rather than one large one. The ideal number for a *Speak, My Soul* group would be a minimum of three and a maximum of eight. While the intent is not to make this an exclusive or closed group, creating a safe place where all voices are heard happens best in smaller numbers. New groups can be formed and facilitated as there is interest.

Listening Group Covenant: At the start of your group, share the following group covenant as the common ground of agreement for how the group will participate together and as a guideline to remind members when the covenant or group norms seem to be ignored.

1. Commit to regularly attend the group as a way to express your faithful support of one another in the journey.
2. Keep confidential what is shared in the group.
3. Listen to one another without interrupting. (The group facilitator may interject if time boundaries need to be honored.)
4. Listen prayerfully to how the Spirit is speaking to you individually and collectively.
5. Avoid cross talk and problem-solving (i.e., do not respond to what someone says with your own story or example of how you handled a similar situation).
6. Allow one another to struggle a little as you share challenges. Give one another space and time to express difficult emotions if needed without jumping in to rescue them from what feels uncomfortable.
7. Give room for silent pause without rushing to respond or to fill the silence. The Divine is often at work in the silence.
8. Give everyone an opportunity to speak during the gathering if they choose to. Do not force anyone to share if they choose not to.
9. Hold one another accountable to this covenant.

Active Listening: Active listening is the hallmark of a listening group. It is different from the dynamics of most small groups that we've experienced in church life or other faith communities. This is not a discussion group where we debate or give feedback about every idea that the group brings up. A listening group eliminates "cross talk" which often has good intentions on how to "help" someone by fixing a problem but denies them the opportunity to explore as a means of finding their own path.

Active listening allows each person in the group time to share what is on their mind or heart without being interrupted. You may set time allocations to give everyone the opportunity to share. Active listening allows an individual to work out their own truth without receiving advice or suggestions. Once an individual comes to a stopping point, invite the group to silently pause, honoring what has been shared in prayerful stillness. Getting used to quiet pauses in a group takes some practice, especially since we're taught to fill the silence in social settings. Active listening relies on three elements:

Receiving—Allow an individual to share while the group remains attentive and focused, letting go of distractions. As you listen, notice any themes, repeated words or phrases, body language, or emotions that may call for further exploration.

Reflecting—Reflecting is bringing what has been shared into a silent, prayerful space. As the group silently reflects, listen for any promptings from the Spirit that arise—encouragements, questions, invitations to the speaker to explore further.

Responding—This is not the same as reacting to what has been said. Following the period of silence and reflecting, group members take turns responding to what they heard. They may acknowledge what was shared, the pain of a situation, a strength or gift that is evident. They may ask a curious question that leads the individual to deeper pondering over what they are expressing. The focus should always remain on the individual and their relationship with God and not shift to someone else's story or experience.

Using the Material: The book is set up for seven weeks of group interaction, covering one inner path each week. Encourage individuals to read the short devotional each day and to reflect using the Rest Stop instructions and questions along with a notebook or journal to capture their thoughts, prayers, and their journey with God through the week.

Weekly Group Meeting: The seventh day of each path offers a guide for reflection appropriate to both individuals and groups. This guide (called Soul Talk) provides a way to review and gather all that has been received. The format is similar each week, which makes it easy to facilitate the group interactions. If your group meets for 60 minutes, you might structure your time as follows:

- 5 minutes—Light a candle as a symbolic welcome to the group and acknowledgment of God's presence in your midst. Open the group time with a minute of silent prayer. I often encourage individuals to take a minute of quiet to breathe and center their body, mind, and spirit into the peaceful presence and light of God, to release all that is not needed, to receive all that is being given.

- 10 minutes—Following this opening silence, take time to experience the *lectio divina* (sacred reading) based on the psalm. You or someone you have asked ahead of time can read the psalm aloud. Instruction in this practice is provided in the Soul Talk section each week.
- 40 minutes—Divide the largest block of your time together evenly amongst the participants. Follow the cycle of listening to a group member share, engaging in collective silent reflection, then responding to the group member's sharing. Encourage each individual to use their responses to the daily Rest Stops and the questions and ideas in Soul Talk to guide their sharing.
- 5 minutes—Close by asking each member what gift or grace they would ask of God to continue walking on the sacred path. Then use a simple blessing (*Go in peace*; *God be with you*), or a prayer to close your time together.

Chapter Resources: The following offers additional resources and reflections to support you in leading and facilitating discussion each week.

The Path of Discernment*—Psalm 62, Psalm 139*

We may wonder about hearing God's voice and recognizing the presence of God throughout our daily lives. Questions may begin to arise about how we know God's will and direction as we navigate decisions and look for the holy in the ordinary tasks of the day. This path of discernment is opportunity for great growth in trusting God even amid confusion. In addition to Psalm 62, read Psalm 139. This is the heart of what is known as a Prayer of Examen: "Search me, O God, and know my heart" (v. 23). It is a prayer that invites the Spirit to bring to our mind the events of the day or the week, considering with gratitude those moments that have been life-giving or life-diminishing.

Group Engagement: At the close of your time together, give each member a 3 x 5 index card. Ask each person to identify something they are currently discerning, an area of their life or a decision they are facing. This may be a major decision they are grappling with or simply discerning God's presence each day. Have them write their area of discernment on the card. Then have them exchange cards with the person on their left or right, and ask each person to pray for the one whose card they hold throughout the coming week.

***The Path of Discipline**—Psalm 63:1-6, 2 Peter 1:3-8*

Reread the introductory thoughts to this chapter that help differentiate what spiritual discipline is and what it is not. Also read 2 Peter 1:3-8 that speaks of participating in the "divine nature" and then lists the ways or disciplines that can nurture this spiritual growth offered by God. This passage is a good reminder that spiritual development and disciplines are a process and are always changing as we grow. Disciplines are not intended to be prescriptive guidelines for the spiritual journey but rather descriptive expressions for the longing of the heart.

Group Engagement: Consider starting a gratitude journal for the group that will become part of a spiritual discipline for the group to experience together. The journal can stay with whomever is leading or facilitating the group. Open the journal each week and encourage individuals to write out their gratitude as they arrive. Alternatively, allow for a few minutes of quiet meditation to reflect on gratitude at the end of your session. Then pass the journal around giving individuals time to record their thoughts. This journal can become a good reflection tool for closing out the group at the end of your time together.

***The Path of Abiding**—Psalm 84, John 15:1-16*

In addition to Psalm 84, take time to read and meditate on John 15:1-16, which records Jesus' words to his disciples about the branches abiding in the vine. Depending on the Bible translation you use, the word *abide* may be translated as "remain" or "dwell." Notice the connection to abiding in Christ and our ability to produce fruit. What does producing fruit represent in the Christian life? What is the connection between abiding and prayer? How does Jesus communicate the intimacy of abiding in him?

Group Engagement: Search online for a version of the hymn "Abide with Me" to play as an opening or closing prayer for your group. If your group is musically inclined, bring copies of the words or music to sing together.

The Path in the Wilderness*—Psalm 77, Luke 7:18-23*

Just as we are enjoying the reality of a dynamic relationship with God, those of us on the spiritual path often reach a point where it all seems to evaporate, or we encounter a great shift in thinking and attitude that leaves us wondering if there isn't more to the journey. Some experience this wilderness as "hitting a wall" that they just can't seem to get around. Others throughout history have called it the "dark night of the soul," where God and all signs of knowing God seem absent. This may have been the situation for John the Baptist. He spent his life and ministry pointing others to Jesus. Yet while he was in prison he seemed to lose sight of Jesus as Messiah. He sends word to Jesus to ask if he really is the Son of God (see Luke 7:18-23). But this wilderness may best be expressed in the simple words of Jesus from the cross: "My God, my God, why have you forsaken me?" (Mark 15:34). Even when all seems lost, we move forward in faith and hope as we wait on God. Explore for yourself and with the group what it means to wait on God—especially when God seems silent.

Group Engagement: If weather permits, consider holding your gathering outdoors to be more in touch with the natural landscape, whatever it is in the area where you live. Let it be an opportunity for each member to express how they would describe the current landscape of their own soul.

The Path of Identity*—Psalm 51, 2 Samuel 12:1–15, Genesis 3*

In coming to know ourselves, we come to know God. But sometimes it takes going through the wilderness or being shocked by our false identity. When the prophet Nathan confronts King David about his infidelity with Bathsheba (see 2 Sam. 12), David is shocked by the revelation of his false identity. David's response isn't denial or an attempt to cover up his misdeeds. Rather he demonstrates a humbled, broken-hearted confession recorded in Psalm 51. This inner path redefines who we are as God-imagined beings. It can be both humbling and exhilarating as we explore both our true-self and false-self.

Identity even has the potential to redefine our concept of "sin" beyond the rules of morality. In the story of Creation and the fall of humanity (see Gen. 2–3), we often get hung up on the disobedience of eating fruit from a forbidden tree. But the "real sin" begins in humanity's insistence on making their own rules and defining their own identity. Reaching for the fruit reveals an attitude of "what God provided isn't enough . . . I want more." The willful denial of their God-imaged self results in hiding behind a false identity with self-made fig leaf coverings (see Gen. 3:7). We battle the same temptation today to become self-realized beings of our own making. But just as God provided appropriate coverings for their chosen life beyond the Garden, so too God meets us with grace upon grace wherever we are and journeys with us on the path of finding our true, God-imaged self.

Group Engagement: As you begin your time together, ask everyone to introduce themselves to the group without using roles, accomplishments, or relationships as part of the description.

The Path of Community*—Psalm 103, John 17*

As much as we've explored the sacred inner path, ultimately our inward journey leads us out again. Near the end of Jesus' earthly life, he prays for his followers—for each of us—to live in the unity of love in Christ and together as a community (see John 17). It's an intense prayer that calls us to live together in the midst of a challenging world. This chapter invites us to consider our worship together, how to bear with one another when things get difficult, and how we might reimagine our faith communities to more fully support one another on the journey.

Group Engagement: Ask the group to think of a word or a phrase that describes their experience of community. Remember, this sharing isn't for others to agree or disagree. The group is to simply hold the word and thoughts shared with welcoming grace. What does community feel like, look like, sound like? Or what is a symbol or metaphor that might offer an image of community?

The Path of Contemplation*—Psalm 131, Psalm 46*

What do we mean by a contemplative life? It is a God-ward life, a prayerful life, attentive to the Divine who is present and at work in the ordinary corners of life. Contemplation is nourished by silence and stillness. It is the lived experience of Psalm 46:10 that says, "Be still, and know that I am God!" It allows for margins of quiet around activities of the day, time to pause, time to work and live at a slower pace than what the world sometimes demands. When we live as a contemplative presence in the world, we live in contentment and offer these gifts to others. The path of contemplation seeks out the life-giving invitations from God. It welcomes the ordinary moments, the joy-filled moments, and even the pain and loss that we inevitably face.

Contemplative living releases the striving that may have defined our earlier faith experiences, and it rests in what is given to do each day. It intimately trusts that God sees and knows and hears all that we encounter and meets us there in love. The contemplative life becomes a more integrated and less fractured life. More God-within, less God-out-there.

Group Engagement: Explore what it would mean for you or your group to live a contemplative life. What would change or shift? What would you need to embrace or release?

Ending Your Group

You may want to have your group meet one additional week to bring closure to all that you've shared together. If desired, include a shared meal or even a Eucharist service. Be creative and ask the group for input on how they would like to close the group. Some suggestions include the following:

1. Ask each person to write a prayer or blessing for the group and to share it.
2. If you kept a group gratitude journal as suggested in week two's Group Engagement activity, read back through it together, having volunteers read a few of the entries until all have been read. Ask how this practice and the messages have impacted each individual.
3. Have each person bring a symbol of the journey you've traveled together to talk about in the last session.
4. Ask each member to share what they have received and what they have released as a result of this inner journey.
5. If desired, ask everyone to come with ideas on how to continue the group on a weekly or monthly basis, either with other new material or as an accountability listening group.

End your time together either in a time of prayer or by reading the closing blessing of compiled psalms found in the epilogue.

APPENDIX 2

ADDITIONAL PSALMS

In addition to the seven psalms that provided focus and foundation to each of the inner path chapters, there are a multitude of other psalms that give dialogue to the soul that you may want to explore either on your own or with a group. These psalms are listed below, along with a few questions and suggestions for reflection and prayer.

Psalm 30—Raising Up the Soul from the Pit

When have you experienced deep sadness or mourning? How did you experience God's presence with you? How did you experience God turning your "mourning into dancing" or exchanging your sackcloth for clothes of joy? How did and do you hold both the mourning and the joy together?

Psalm 34—The Soul Magnifies the Lord

This psalm recounts the ways that God responded to David during times of trouble. What might your own psalm sound like as you recall the ways God has blessed you? How does this recounting enlarge or magnify your view of the Lord?

Psalm 42—The Soul Longs for God

When your soul is downcast, disquieted, or restless within, what do you long for? What do you thirst for in these times? As you read through this psalm, which words resonate with you? In what ways do you relate to the psalmist?

Psalm 57—Awake My Soul

How has your soul awakened to new ideas and possibilities as you've explored your sacred path within? Where do you notice your soul feeling lethargic or sleepy? How might you turn this awakening or desire for awakening into a prayer?

Psalm 86—An Undivided Heart and Soul

In times of trouble, David turns heart and soul to the only one who hears and answers when he feels "poor and needy" (v. 1). Then he asks God for specific graces to see him through. What graces do you want to ask of God when you feel poor and needy?

Psalm 119—The Soul Melts

Psalm 119 is the longest chapter in all scripture. Take time to read through it during the day or over a week. Listen for how it speaks to your soul. Note specifically verses 25-32, 81-83, and 169-176.

APPENDIX 3
A LENTEN RETREAT

Lent is the forty days preceding Easter in which Christians often choose to faithfully make a spiritual pilgrimage of the heart with Jesus as we remember his approach to the end of his earthly life. Lent is typically filled with acts of devotion and sacrifice, liturgies practiced in community, and prayers offered in the private place and time set aside to turn body, heart, mind, and spirit toward these days of passion and suffering.

Because of its seven-week format, *Speak, My Soul* could be a good companion on the inner path with Jesus during Lent. You may choose to do so in a variety of ways. I offer three suggestions that you can use or adapt to your own rhythm, pace, and intention during this season.

Retreat #1: Lent in Community

If you're meeting with a group to work through this material together, consider beginning the readings one week prior to Ash Wednesday, the beginning of Lent on the liturgical calendar. Use the instructions outlined in appendix 1 for instructions on leading a group through this book and specifics on how to use your time each week as you meet together. Members of the group commit to reading daily during the week leading up to the meeting; coming prepared to share what their journey has been like during the week; and being open to the invitations, challenges, or transformations that have come as a result of the reading.

As group members read and meditate on the devotional, they are creating a mini-retreat on their own in ten to twenty minutes each day. Each weekly meeting is another extended retreat with the group in a sixty-to-ninety-minute session. In addition to this daily and weekly rhythm of retreat, consider an extended daily time of prayer and devotion during Holy Week (Palm Sunday through Easter Sunday) and devoting additional time daily to meditating on the Word, in the silence, in prayer, and on the passion of Jesus.

Retreat #2: A Concentrated Personal Retreat

The point of retreat is to come away from your normal routines and to offer yourself wholeheartedly to God. You can design a "retreat" in any style you desire as described below. Choose any one of the seven "sacred paths" as your focus during your retreat. Depending on the time you have set aside, select readings to align with your schedule. Whether you use all seven readings or only two or three is up to you and the time you have available. Plan to spend an hour or two with each meditation you choose to include in your retreat. If you have a longer time frame of multiple days away be sure you attend to body, mind, and spirit.

For each session of your retreat, use the following pattern to spend time with each chosen meditation.

1. **Prepare**. Before sitting down to pray, read, and meditate, take time to prepare your body for your journey. Take a short walk or do some stretching exercises. Brew a cup of tea or coffee and settle into your retreat space.
2. **Pray.** Consider writing your intention for this retreat time as a prayer in your journal. What do you ask of God for this retreat? How might God offer a blessing to you as you meditate, read, write, think, and move through your set-aside time?

3. **Read** the opening psalm for the selected sacred path and the introductory page. Allow it to turn your heart and spirit toward God and toward your intimate connection with the Divine. Read through the first selected devotional, giving yourself time to meditate on what you've read. Notice if a word or phrase specifically catches your attention or makes you wonder about something in your own soul.
4. **Silence**. Spend a few minutes holding that word or phrase and letting it speak to your soul. After this time of open silent reflection, reread the devotional a second time to seal in your heart what God invites you to consider.
5. **Journal.** Finally, begin to record in your journal a conversation with Jesus about the words you are pondering. What challenges in the words are you holding within you? What invitations are there to godly comfort? What needs to be released to make room for something new? How might you carry these words with you into your everyday life?

Once you've completed the first devotional, take a short break to stretch, to go outside if you've been indoors, or perhaps to turn to an artistic expression of painting, sketching, or collecting found objects during your walk to arrange as an offering of praise to God. Refill your coffee or tea if needed before returning again to the path. When you are ready, re-center yourself and begin the process above with the next devotional reading.

Retreat #3: Walking with Jesus

Consider developing a Lenten retreat using the sixth reading from each of the seven chapters, which focuses on an aspect of the final days of Jesus' life on earth—from the upper room to Gethsemane, the trial, the crucifixion and burial, the resurrection, and beyond. Those seven readings include the following:

- The Shadow of the Cross (page 23)

Divide the readings evenly across your allotted time frame. A seven- or eight-hour retreat would allow you to spend approximately one hour with each devotional. Or choose three or four of the readings and allow two hours for reading, silence, prayer, journaling.

Another approach to this journey with Jesus would be to spread the seven readings out over the seven days leading up to Easter. An hour each morning will allow you to read, meditate, journal, and pray through all seven Lenten devotionals. Use or adapt the format noted in Retreat #2 to help guide you.

APPENDIX 4
THE INNER PATH IDENTIFIERS

Each pathway described in this book provides a new vantage point to the spiritual journey. And each path brings us to unique experiences of growth and transformation. The table below offers a general overview of some of the characteristics an individual may experience on each pathway. Use this tool to identify the pathways where you have walked, where you currently are walking, or where you may expect to explore in the future.

Every individual experiences these paths in their own way based on their history, personality, and, above all, their unique relationship with God. Use this resource to contemplate the ways *you* experience the inner pathways, which may be much different than what you see in the table below. Add your own descriptions, challenges, and disciplines to this table as a reminder of the unique ways the Spirit meets you and speaks to you on these personal pathways divinely paved just for you.

Inner Path	Description / Traits	Challenges / Temptations	Discipline
Discernment	Awakening, listening, transitioning, seeking wisdom	Restlessness, the "right" answer or choice, quick solutions	Prayer of Examen
Discipline	Receptive, humbled, nurtured, spiritually hungry, a sense of growth	Information without transformation, spiritual gluttony	Remember "only one thing is needed"
Abiding	Longing for God, spiritual desire, intimacy with God, centered, resting	Distractions, busyness, boredom	Scripture meditation
Wilderness	Dry, barren, stuck, alone, darkness, waiting, questioning, confusion, trusting	Wandering, seeking ways to escape the wilderness, believing you've lost your way	Stillness, silence, patient waiting
Identity	Releasing / grieving false identities, humility, setting boundaries, new birth, confidence, voice	Defensiveness, denial of false self, confusion	Confession, journaling
Community	Belonging, encouraging, supporting, listening, deconstructing, reimagining	Observing/ judging without connecting or participating	Worship
Contemplation	Freedom, welcome, contentment, attentiveness and comfort in the present moment, acceptance, visions, acknowledgment of your belovedness	Retreat from community or responsibilities, guilt over "wasting time"	Meditation, silence

NOTES

The Path of Discernment

1. Henri Nouwen, *Discernment: Reading the Signs of Daily Life* (New York: HarperOne, 2013), 5–6.

The Path of Abiding

2. Henry F. Lyte, *Abide with Me*, 1847, Copyright status Public Domain. (United Methodist Hymnal, 1989), 700.
3. Richard J. Foster, *Prayer: Finding the Heart's True Home* (New York: HarperCollins, 1992), 1.

The Path of Wilderness

4. Brother Lawrence, *The Practice of the Presence of God* (Grand Rapids, MI: Spire Books, 2007), 30.

The Path of Identity

5. Martin Laird, *Into the Silent Land: A Guide to the Christian Practice of Contemplation* (New York: Oxford University Press, 2006), 91.

The Path of Community

6. You can read more about spiritual direction in my book *Sacred Conversation: Exploring the Seven Gifts of Spiritual Direction* (Nashville, TN: Upper Room Books, 2022), or at www.marshacrockett.org .

For those who hunger for deep spiritual experience . . .

The Academy for Spiritual Formation® is an experience of disciplined Christian community emphasizing holistic spirituality—nurturing body, mind, and spirit. The program, a ministry of The Upper Room®, is ecumenical in nature and meant for all those who hunger for a deeper relationship with God, including both lay and clergy persons. Each Academy fosters spiritual rhythms—of study and prayer, silence and liturgy, solitude and relationship, rest and play.

With offerings of both Two-Year and Five-Day models, Academy participants rediscover Christianity's rich spiritual heritage through worship, learning, and fellowship. During the Two-Year Academy, pilgrims gather at a retreat center for five days every three months over the course of two years (a total of 40 days), and the Five-Day Academy is a modified version of the Two-Year experience, inviting pilgrims to gather for five days of spiritual learning and worship. The Academy's commitment to an authentic spirituality promotes balance, inner and outer peace, holy living and justice living—God's shalom.

Faculty trained in the wide breadth of Christian spirituality and practice provide content and guidance at each session of The Academy. Academy faculty presenters come from seminaries, monasteries, spiritual direction ministries, and pastoral ministries or other settings and are from a variety of traditions.

The Academy Recommends program seeks to highlight content that aligns with the Academy's mission to create transformative space for people to connect with God, self, others, and creation for the sake of the world.

Learn more by visiting academy.upperroom.org.

Printed in the USA
CPSIA information can be obtained
at www.ICGtesting.com
LVHW010859200424
777878LV00013B/1111

9 780835 820592